AT THE GLOBAL CROSSROADS

At the Global Crossroads

The Sylvia Ostry Foundation Lectures

Published for the Institute for Research on Public Policy
by
McGill-Queen's University Press
Montreal & Kingston · London · Ithaca

ISBN 0-7735-2637-4

Legal deposit fourth quarter 2003
Bibliothèque nationale du Québec

Printed in Canada on acid-free paper.

This book has been published with the help of grants from the Institute for Research on Public Policy and the Sylvia Ostry Foundation.

Publishing consultant: Malcolm Lester & Associates

McGill-Queen's University Press acknowledges the support of the Canada Council for the Arts for our publishing program.

National Library of Canada Cataloguing in Publication

At the global crossroads : The Sylvia Ostry Foundation lectures.
Series of 6 lectures given between 1993 and 2002.
ISBN 0-7735-2637-4
1. International economic relations – Congresses. 2. Economic development – Congresses. 3. Globalization – Economic aspects – Congresses. I. Institute for Research on Public Policy. II. Title: The Sylvia Ostry Foundation lectures.
HF1359.A9 2003 337 C2003-903147-0

Typeset in Palatino 10.5/14
by Caractéra inc., Quebec City

Contents

Foreword ix
MICHAEL WILSON

Introduction xi
PETER G. WHITE

Challenge to the United Nations: A Humanitarian Perspective 3
SADAKO OGATA

The Future of Europe: Managing Economic and Social Change 17
JACQUES DELORS

The International Monetary Fund in a Globalized World Economy: The Tasks Ahead 34
MICHEL CAMDESSUS

The Road Ahead: International Trade Policy in the Era of the World Trade Organization 49
RENATO RUGGIERO

Prospects for Greater Hemispheric Economic Cooperation: An Opportunity for Canada 68
ENRIQUE V. IGLESIAS

International Financial Markets: The Prospects for Economic Growth and Stability 85
PAUL VOLCKER

Contributors 99

The Institute for Research on Public Policy is honoured to co-publish the Sylvia Ostry Foundation Lectures. Sylvia Ostry's work represents the highest standards of scholarship, international policy knowledge, and public service. Her academic and public service contributions are seminal to the direction and substance of much of what is right and good about Canadian trade and economic policy. These lectures initiated in her honour reflect not only the breadth of her interests, her linkages and her skills, but also her amazing conceptual and intellectual depth.

In the IRPP's early years Dr Ostry served as a distinguished fellow. Through this collaboration the organization benefited immensely from her skills, insights, and wisdom.

The IRPP is Canada's oldest nonpartisan, bilingual public policy research institute. It was established in 1972 through an independent endowment consisting of public sector, corporate, foundation, and individual contributions. Its mission is to inform and enhance public policy outcomes and debate in Canada through empirical research, accessible publications, working papers, symposia, and conferences.

Hugh Segal
President, IRPP
(www.irpp.org)

Foreword

When Bernard Ostry asked me to succeed Peter White as chair of the Sylvia Ostry Foundation, I was intrigued. I had worked with Sylvia on a number of occasions during my time in public office and had tremendous admiration for the work that she did, particularly at the pressure-packed G7 Summits. I was also interested in finding out who had given the Sylvia Ostry Lectures since the inception of the foundation. The list that Bernard produced for me was very impressive indeed. These were lectures on matters of great current interest by clear leaders in their respective fields. Given my career in public and political service, I readily accepted the opportunity and honour of being chair of the Sylvia Ostry Foundation.

My first task was to invite my friend Paul Volcker to deliver the most recent lecture. Barbara McDougall, president of the Canadian Institute for International Affairs, and I agreed that collaboration between the Foundation and the CIIA was important in order to establish a sound base for these lectures in the future. This collaboration started with the Volcker lecture and promises to be a productive partnership for future lectures.

The success that Peter and his colleagues had achieved since establishing the Foundation was impressive. It was clearly important to continue this tradition, both to honour Sylvia and to bring this calibre of individual to Canada to speak. It was also important to make these lectures part of a permanent record. Hence this book.

Michael Wilson
Chair
The Sylvia Ostry Foundation

Introduction

I have had the pleasure of knowing Dr Sylvia Ostry and her husband, Bernard, since 1963. At that time I was an assistant to the Honourable Maurice Sauvé in Ottawa where the Ostry's were a power couple long before the term was coined. So when Bernard, that tireless promoter of his wife's causes, asked me one day in 1991 to take on the chairmanship of the Sylvia Ostry Foundation, I agreed immediately.

The Sylvia Ostry Foundation was established in April 1991 by a number of Sylvia's Canadian friends and admirers. Its object was to sponsor a major annual or biennial lecture in Canada on a subject related to the global economic and financial system. In the words of William A. Macdonald, who announced the project at a dinner in Sylvia's honour in Ottawa on 19 April 1991, the lectureship was modeled on the Per Jacobsson lectures in Washington, which were established in 1964 under the auspices of the International Monetary Fund in Washington and the Bank for International Settlements in Basle, Switzerland. This was a fitting model for two reasons. First, Sylvia Ostry had delivered the 1987 Per Jacobsson lecture, establishing her credentials. She was in the company of other distinguished

Per Jacobsson lecturers such as Gerald Bouey and Paul Volcker. Second, Sylvia had long insisted that we in Canada lived in a global economy and "had better learn to act accordingly."

The launch of the Sylvia Ostry Foundation also marked Sylvia's elevation in 1990 to the level of Companion of the Order of Canada. Since then the trustees have sought outstanding speakers on topics related to Sylvia's professional interests, which gave us a wide scope indeed.

It is not a simple matter to persuade eminent thinkers to take time to prepare a full-dress lecture and then spend a day travelling to Ottawa or Toronto to deliver it. But Sylvia has many non-Canadian friends and admirers in high places and a gratifying number of them have been delighted to accept our invitation. This volume reproduces the first six Sylvia Ostry Lectures. The first four lectures were given in Ottawa, and the last two in Toronto. All have dealt with particular aspects of Sylvia's work – especially perhaps her participation in meetings of the leaders of the G7-G8 nations.

The inaugural lecture was given in May 1993 by Sadako Ogata, United Nations High Commissioner for Refugees, who highlighted three issues: problems in protecting millions of displaced persons affected by conflict in their own country; use of an international presence to protect such persons, and the importance of humanitarian access and military force to ensure it.

Mrs Ogata was followed in April 1994 by Jacques Delors, president of the European Commission. At a time of almost worldwide recession, M Delors addressed the "European disease," asking whether this was a disorder of industrial societies in general, perhaps arising from globalization or whether we are undergoing a radical change in the world we have known since 1945. He also stressed the importance of European security.

Michel Camdessus, managing director of the International Monetary Fund, spoke in June 1995. His theme was the upcoming twenty-first summit of the industrial countries in Naples. He identified four challenges for the twenty-first century: improving trade relations, helping developing countries, progress in transitional economies, and market stabilization.

The fourth lecture was given by Renato Ruggiero, director general of the World Trade Organization, in May 1996. Mr Ruggiero urged further liberalization for trade in goods and services, multilateral rules for investment and trade, better competition policy, trade and labour standards, and more work on curbing corruption, and on government procurement, regionalism, and trade earnings in developing countries.

Because of scheduling problems, the next lecture was not held until April 2000, when the speaker was Enrique V. Iglesias, president of the Inter-American Development Bank. Mr Iglesias reviewed Canada's recent relations with Latin America and our immense mutual opportunities. Key challenges he noted were dispute settlement procedures and the need for institutional infrastructure and technical support.

The last lecture was given by Paul Volcker, former chair of the US Federal Reserve Board, in October 2002. In a time of international financial crises, Mr Volcker spoke of the need to test the model of democratic capitalism in creating a truly globalized economy. He called for examination of obstacles to emerging economies. In touching on those matters, Mr Volcker argued the need for increased financial integration and an overhaul of the existing exchange rate system. He emphasized the potential for direct investment in emerging economies and, above all, the need for reform in corporate governance, financial reporting, and executive compensation practices in North America and Europe.

The Sylvia Ostry Foundation has been generously endowed by many corporations and individuals, as well as by the federal government. While we cannot mention every donor, I would like to recognize the initial gifts of Labatts, Power Corporation, Bank of

Montreal, BCE, and Harrison McCain, which brought the infant foundation into being.

For some years we engaged the Public Policy Forum in Ottawa to help with the physical arrangements. More recently, we have teamed up with the Canadian Institute of International Affairs in Toronto. The Department of External Affairs (now DFAIT) kindly held a special dinner in the Pearson Building for each lecturer who visited Ottawa.

I want to especially thank Bernard Ostry for ensuring that these lectures were collected in book form.

Finally, I want to thank the Institute for Research on Public Policy for "partnering" with us to publish this book. It is under their auspices that McGill-Queen's is bringing the book to publication.

It was at a CIIA lunch in Toronto in October 2002 that Peter Peterson, former US secretary of Commerce, told how President Kennedy's speechwriter Ted Sorenson had recently described a friend's new volume, with tongue in cheek, as "the kind of book that, once you have put it down, you will never want to pick it up again."

Having been present at all these lectures, I think I can assure you that this is not such a book.

Peter G. White
Chair, 1991–2002
The Sylvia Ostry Foundation

AT THE GLOBAL CROSSROADS

Challenge to the United Nations
A Humanitarian Perspective

SADAKO OGATA

It was a great privilege and pleasure for me to present the inaugural lecture of the Sylvia Ostry Foundation. Dr Ostry is one of those rare individuals who has been able to combine practical experience of international and domestic policy-making with academic research covering macro and micro economic issues. During her distinguished career, Mrs Ostry has been a powerful and persuasive advocate of coordinated international policies and freer multinational trade.

Enormous challenges have been posed to the United Nations in the post-Cold War era, particularly from a humanitarian perspective. I hope to examine the ways in which humanitarian issues have become linked with the efforts of the United Nations to establish peace and security and to reflect on the inter-relationship between humanitarian and political action as the United Nations strives to bring order to a world in transition.

We are living in a period of rapid change, in which international security has become more complex and national boundaries more permeable and mutable. On the positive side, adversarial attitudes of the Cold War have been replaced by a new willingness to cooperate. The reduction of East/West tensions has led to the resolution of many regional and internal conflicts and disputes. From Central Europe to Latin America, from Thailand to Mali, old assumptions and structures are being challenged and authoritarianism is giving way, in varying degrees, to more democratic forms of government and more open economies. Trade and commerce, modern transport and communications are blurring national boundaries, just as global concerns about drugs, AIDS, environmental degradation, and international migration are drawing governments together into new forms of cooperation.

On the negative side, political and economic reform is proving to be a painful, sometimes violent process, as shown in Haiti, Zaire, and other parts of the world. Underlying these political conflicts or independent of them, ancient feuds are being rekindled by nationalistic, ethnic, cultural, and religious rivalries, leading to violence, sometimes culminating in the fragmentation of states, as in the former Soviet Union and Yugoslavia. Within these "new" states, more seeds of strife are being sown among insecure minorities. The former Yugoslavia provides a particularly graphic and painful example – but unfortunately not the only one – of the atrocious policy of torture, rape, and murder used to force one group of people to leave territory shared with another. Wars, which were previously fuelled by the superpowers, are continuing even after the withdrawal of their patrons. In Somalia, and to a large extent also in Afghanistan, violence and anarchy have destroyed any semblance of governmental authority. These dangerous and destabilizing trends could have repercussions far beyond the borders of the conflict-ridden countries. Even in those countries, such as Cambodia and Angola, where the end of the Cold War had led to the settlement of internal wars, a new period of uncertainty is demonstrating the fragility of the peace process. The United Nations has engaged in heroic efforts in these countries to maintain peace and order while attempting to establish democratically elected governments.

Political instability is feeding and, in turn, is itself being exacerbated by the problems of poverty, growing population pressures, and environmental degradation which, of course, pre-date the end of the Cold War. At the same time, the relationship between North and South is being challenged in a world in which the division between East and West is gradually disappearing. Countries that have lost their strategic use as superpower pawns find themselves largely ignored by their former patrons. Furthermore, in many industrialized countries, public support for foreign-aid programs is becoming difficult to sustain in the midst of prolonged economic recession.

On the humanitarian scene, large-scale refugee movements and population displacement are being generated by political and ethnic conflicts. The world refugee population grew from some 13 million in 1989 to almost 19 million in 1993. In the course of 1992 alone, my office mounted emergency programs for 3.8 million people in the former Yugoslavia, for some 260,000 refugees from Myanmar in Bangladesh, and 420,000 refugees in Kenya, mainly from Somalia. In early December 1992 we sent emergency teams to Armenia, Azerbaijan, and Tajikistan and have had to cope with the influx of some 200,000 refugees from Togo into Benin and Ghana.

People are being forced not only to cross borders and become refugees but also are being displaced inside their own countries. The conflict in Tajikistan in 1992 produced 500,000 internally displaced persons as well as 60,000 refugees who crossed into Afghanistan. Violence and anarchy in Somalia caused some one million refugees to flee to the neighbouring countries and another million to become internally displaced. In Mozambique there were 3 million internally displaced persons in addition to about 1.5 million refugees in Malawi and other African countries. In Bosnia-Herzegovina, about 2 million people became dependent on international assistance through being internally displaced or having to survive in besieged cities. In addition, over a million refugees were in Croatia, Serbia, and other neighbouring countries.

In the face of such political instability, economic uncertainty, and humanitarian crises, the euphoria that greeted the end of the Cold War was overtaken by a sober reassessment of the new geopolitical realities. The risk in the mid 1990s seems not so much that of hegemonic dominance but more of the consequences of its absence, with no superpower willing or able to impose order. Major countries are turning inwards and are preoccupied with domestic concerns. Against this background of a power vacuum, the United Nations is increasingly expected to contain and control conflicts. How can the United Nations be strengthened to allow it to perform its primary responsibility of maintaining international peace and security? How should the United Nations balance the principle of non-interference in the internal affairs of the state with the need to address threats to international peace and security that result more and more from internal conflicts? How does an organization like the United Nations High Commission for Refugees (UNHCR), whose mandate was carefully crafted to respect state sovereignty by providing international protection and assistance to refugees only after they have left their own country, respond to the humanitarian needs of those who have been displaced but are still within their national borders?

These are enormous challenges for a United Nations stultified by four decades of Cold War. In a bipolar world, it was not possible to eliminate the root causes of refugee movements because they clearly derived from ideological and political confrontation. Peacekeeping operations tended to freeze the frontlines but let the conflicts fester, while humanitarian action took care of the refugees but immobilized refugee situations for decades, e.g., in Mozambique, Afghanistan, and Cambodia. Humanitarian action on behalf of refugees was undertaken without reference to the political situations that had given rise to the refugee flow. UNHCR's mandate was interpreted as protection of refugees after they had left their country. Prevention and solutions were considered to be beyond UNHCR's area of competence. By focusing on asylum and the maintenance of refugee camps across the border, attention was deflected from the country of origin, where the source – and hence the solution – of most refugee problems lay. Yet there was little else that UNHCR could do, in the absence of the political will to allow the United Nations to prevent conflicts, not to speak of tackling the root cause that led to refugee flows.

In 1993, the static framework of the Cold War has been replaced by a more dynamic situation, in which the risks of conflicts and refugees flows have been revived but, equally, the opportunities to address them have been renewed. *An Agenda for Peace*, the report put forward by the UN Secretary-General in 1992, advocates an active engagement by the United Nations to ensure world security through preventive diplomacy, peace-making or conflict resolution, peacekeeping and peace-building, or post-conflict rehabilitation. There is clearly a new readiness in the Security Council to examine internal situations and civil wars as threats to international peace and security. There is a new emphasis on early warning and preventive action, as shown by the preventive deployment of peacekeepers to Macedonia last December. New demands are being put on the United Nations, as peace becomes a multi-dimensional concept in a complex security framework. In countries as far apart as Namibia and Nicaragua, El Salvador and Angola, Cambodia and Mozambique, Somalia, former Yugoslavia, and Tajikistan, the UN is brokering peace, supervising ceasefires, demobilizing soldiers, assisting refugees to return, monitoring elections, promoting human rights, and protecting the delivery of humanitarian assistance.

These developments have had enormous implications for my office. New imperatives and new opportunities are defining a post–Cold War strategy for humanitarian action. Like the new generation of peacekeepers, humanitarian action is having to focus on internal rather than intra-state problems, whether in the context of returning refugees – who numbered around 1.5 million in 1992 – or internally displaced persons. This means not only responding to refugee situations in countries of asylum, but also preventing and resolving them in the countries from which refugees originate. We must seek to ensure that people are not forced to flee their homes in the first place but, if they are, then their humanitarian needs must be met and conditions created to allow them to return home in safety and dignity. In order to cope with the changing realities, I adopted a three-pronged strategy of prevention, preparedness, and solutions. It is an attempt to complement the existing assurance of asylum *outside* the country of origin with prevention and solution-oriented activities *inside* the country of origin.

As the focus of our activities shifts gradually from the relatively stable conditions in the country of asylum to the more turbulent and often evolutionary process in the country of origin, it becomes more and more linked to the political efforts of the United Nations to bring about peace and security. Nowhere has this been more clearly demonstrated than in the former Yugoslavia where humanitarian operations are working closely, on the one hand, with the political process of the International Conference co-chaired by Mr Vance (replaced by Mr. Stoltenberg) and Lord Owen, and on the other, with the UN peacekeeping mission on the ground.

It is clear that the implications and inter-relationships between political and humanitarian action are as complex as implementation problems are manifold. Let me point out three main issues.

The first relates to the political and legal problems of *protecting displaced people* in their own country who are affected by conflict. Unlike refugee law, humanitarian law, specifically the Geneva Conventions and Protocol II, contains provisions for the protection of civilians in internal armed conflicts, which are of great value to the internally displaced. These provisions do not, however, apply to situations of internal disturbances and tensions, such as riots, and isolated and sporadic acts of violence, which often cause people to flee.

Thus it is left to human rights law to provide the necessary protection to internally displaced persons. Yet many human rights are subject to derogation during a period of public emergency, exactly at a time when the need to protect the displaced is the greatest. This is a lacuna in humanitarian and human rights law that needs to be addressed.

In addition to the legal gap, the framework for the protection and assistance of the internally displaced is unclear because of the sensitivities of national sovereignty. Protection of the human rights of an individual within his or her national territory is premised on state responsibility. This responsibility devolves on the country of origin by virtue of fundamental state obligations to safeguard and protect its citizens. However, in a situation of internal displacement, the state may itself be the persecutor or may be unwilling to protect or even be unable to do so, for instance if it has lost territorial control during an armed conflict. The international human rights machinery is currently far from adequate in addressing such situations. The assumption of national sovereignty traditionally leaves no international jurisdiction for protection, unlike that of UNHCR in the case of refugees. However, the growing recognition of legitimate international concern about human rights matters is slowly creating more space for international bodies to play a role in monitoring the protection of the internally displaced than was previously considered possible.

As part of our strategy to prevent refugee problems and address them *before* people cross the border, and at the request of the secretary-general and the government concerned, UNHCR has undertaken an active role for the protection and assistance of internally displaced people, for instance in Sri Lanka, Tajikistan, and the former Yugoslavia. We have also launched an innovative operation in Somalia from across the border in Kenya so that people are not forced to leave their country solely for lack of international assistance. This is an effort to provide assistance in the country of origin close to the border where security conditions are satisfactory. Such an operation is not only preventive in terms of future movements but also encourages refugees who have left the area to return as soon as security conditions permit. When refugees choose to return to areas where there are internally displaced persons, UNHCR has sought to assist both groups, in an effort to stabilize communities and promote an early durable solution. This is our approach in Afghanistan, Angola, and the Horn of Africa.

The war in Bosnia-Herzegovina has added a new category to our list of beneficiaries. These are people who are under siege or otherwise being pressurized to move but have not yet been displaced. Assisting people to remain where they are is an important – indeed crucial – function in a war, the primary objective of which seems to be the expulsion of minority groups. Normally such activities are carried out by the International Committee of the Red Cross, but are now falling also to UNHCR as the UN becomes more engaged in internal conflict situations. Thus mandates and modes of cooperation are developing out of the operational realities with which we are being daily confronted.

My second point is about the use of *international presence* as a tool for protecting internally displaced persons. For instance, UNHCR has set up Open Relief Centres in northern Sri Lanka which are accepted and respected by both warring parties as havens of safety for displaced persons, although the centres have no legal status as such. Political developments permitting, UNHCR is negotiating a humanitarian corridor for the free movement of the civilian population in northern Sri Lanka.

Elsewhere, massive presence in the context of an assistance program can act as a confidence-building measure to enhance security. During 1991 and 1992 in northern Iraq, UNHCR deployed some 180 staff, augmented by hundreds of NGOs and the innovative use of some 500 UN guards. In Bosnia-Herzegovina, in 1993, there are some 600 UNHCR staff, who not only help to distribute relief to the displaced and besieged but also monitor their protection situation. There are some 7,000 UN peacekeeping forces to protect relief activities. In the context of current realities in Bosnia, international presence, accompanied by massive life-sustaining assistance, may be the only practical form of protection for the besieged population.

On 16 April 1993, the Security Council adopted a resolution (SC res. 819) requesting the secretary-general to increase the presence of UN peacekeeping troops in Srebrenica town, the centre of Muslim besieged enclaves in Eastern Bosnia in order to monitor the humanitarian situation. The Council demanded that all parties treat Srebrenica as a "safe area" free from armed attack or other hostile acts. In part thanks to the able Canadian peacekeepers, the safe-area concept is largely being respected. The safe-area concept as it is evolving in Bosnia-Herzegovina is that of population centres that are being placed under international protection, with the UN presence of peacekeepers and humanitarian organizations to provide relief. As the Security Council expands the designation of safe areas to Zepa, Gorazde, Tuzla, and Sarajevo, a new humanitarian approach may be developing that links the protection of civilians more directly in the process towards achieving final peace. Safe areas, of course, should not turn into large-scale refugee camps.

Generally speaking, UN humanitarian organizations have obtained access and established presence on the basis of negotiations and consent of the parties. This is also true so far of the situation in Bosnia-Herzegovina. However, there is now a growing debate on the use of force to obtain access. My third point, therefore, is about *humanitarian access* and the use of military force to ensure such access. You will recall that on 5 April 1991 the Security Council created a precedent by adopting Resolution 688, linking human rights violations to threats to international peace and security. The resolution demanded that Iraq allow immediate access by international humanitarian organizations to all those in need of assistance in all parts of Iraq. The day after the resolution was adopted, the Coalition forces intervened militarily to create a safety zone in northern Iraq. This helped to protect those who could not obtain asylum in Turkey. It was a clear indication that the issue of humanitarian access challenged the traditional inviolability of national sovereignty. Interestingly enough, UNHCR's activities in northern Iraq were not based on Resolution 688, nor on the Coalition intervention, but on a memorandum of understanding negotiated between the United Nations and the government of Iraq. There is, of course, no doubt that the adoption of Resolution 688 and the apparent determination of the international community to enforce it influenced the outcomes of the negotiations.

UNHCR's involvement in the former Yugoslavia pre-dates the deployment of peacekeeping forces. It came about as a result of a request from the then-Yugoslav government and from the United Nations secretary-general to protect and assist persons displaced by the war in Croatia. Very soon after, following the independence of Croatia, UNHCR was involved not only in helping internally displaced persons but also refugees who crossed into or found themselves in what became Croatia and the rump Yugoslavia. In the spring of 1992, when the fighting spread to Bosnia-Herzegovina, ensuring humanitarian access to Sarajevo and other besieged cities became a major issue. In Bosnia-Herzegovina, Security Council Resolution 716 of 29 June 1992 authorized the United Nations Protection Force (UNPROFOR) to protect Sarajevo airport and access to the city so that UNHCR could continue to protect and assist those in need. Through Security Council Resolution 776 of 14 September 1992, UNPROFOR's mandate was extended to support UNHCR's humanitarian activities and provide military cover to relief convoys. Although existing rules of engagement allow UN peacekeeping forces to open fire if armed persons attempt by force to prevent them from carrying out their orders, the protection and delivery of humanitarian assistance by UNPROFOR have so far been based on consensual arrangements with the parties involved.

Obtaining consent can be difficult not only because of governmental intransigence but also because of the multiplicity in the command structure – civilian, military, and even local warlords. Frequently, the chain of command is unclear and discipline weak, making negotiations, whether on ceasefires or humanitarian access, difficult and dangerous. This has certainly been the case in Bosnia-Herzegovina, where the UNPROFOR and UNHCR staff have spent an inordinate amount of time and effort to gain assurances, only to have them broken as soon as our convoys begin rolling. Despite all the problems, I would like to emphasize the importance of negotiations and consensus-building as the final tool to establish trust and confidence of all parties concerned as the essential condition for carrying out humanitarian work.

The humanitarian imperative requires impartial support to victims on all sides of a conflict, while enforcement action by the United Nations must necessarily target the aggressor. There could thus be at least a potential problem for us as the Security Council increasingly undertakes action in situations where there are no longer secure conditions for humanitarian action. It was this type of situation of total breakdown of law and order combined with the starvation of the Somali people that prompted United Nations intervention in Somalia in December 1992. Following the failure of the advance team of peacekeepers to take control over the airport and the seaport to allow delivery of humanitarian assistance, and the continued defiance of the Somali warlords to accept full deployment of the United Nations peacekeepers, the secretary-general recommended to the Security Council to move into enforcement action under Chapter VII of the UN Charter. The secretary-general's judgment was based on the conclusion that Somalia lacked any governmental authority with which to reach agreement, and therefore the United Nations had to forcefully create conditions for the uninterrupted delivery of relief supplies to the starving people.

In the case of Bosnia-Herzegovina, the Bosnian Serbs are yet to accept the peace accord promoted by the co-chairmen of the International Conference on former Yugoslavia. International pressure is mounting for more resolute political and military action to assure ceasefire and compliance of the parties to the UN Peace Plan. The impact of military intervention on the activities of the peacekeeping forces on the ground as well as on humanitarian agencies needs to be cautiously weighed. The dilemma of the international community is this: on the one hand, the protection of the victims of the conflict – refugees, displaced civilians, women, and children – must be scrupulously upheld. On the other hand, the political imperative requires resolute results even at some cost to the victims.

Northern Iraq, the former Yugoslavia, and Somalia have indicated the emergence of the humanitarian domain as a source for Security Council decision-making. However, consensus has yet to emerge on the norms, rules, and decision-making process involving political and military action for humanitarian purposes. As humanitarian action becomes dynamically linked to peacemaking and peacekeeping, principles must be developed to reconcile humanitarian action with Chapter VII enforcement, whether economic, military, or otherwise. I have noted that sanctions too often affect the vulnerable – children, mothers, the aged – before making any impact on the aggressor leadership. UNHCR must make all efforts to ensure that the neutrality, impartiality, and humanitarian nature of its operations that allow it to address the victims on all sides of a conflict are scrupulously upheld.

In the meanwhile it is clear that humanitarian assistance, primarily designed to protect victims, can help defuse tensions as well as contribute to an environment conducive for peace talks. In the Bosnian context, we have sometimes been told that humanitarian assistance has not contributed to peace; that it has merely fed people who will be killed the next day. I cannot categorically refute these allegations as humanitarian activities cannot substitute for political settlement. However, I am proud that humanitarian relief activities have in fact helped to save more than 2 million lives in Bosnia in 1992. This is why I yearn for a speedy cessation of hostilities and political settlement while we carry on our work every day in spite of continued odds. Once a peace settlement is achieved, humanitarian assistance will play a major role to help return refugees and displaced persons and eventually provide a bridge to long-term development.

In conclusion, let me stress that in a world without hegemons, the challenges for the United Nations are manifold. The threats to international peace and security in today's world do not, in most instances, come from outright military aggression across national borders but primarily from the internal situation of sovereign states. The most frequent cases are likely to be caused by misgovernment or disintegration of state power – internal conflicts, breakdown of law and order, collapse of economic and social systems, mass displacement of people. Such threats cannot be dealt with solely as a matter between states, for the issues of today do not arise from nor affect only the relations between states but also those between state and individual, between state and group, and between groups within the states.

The current system of collective security will have to be both reviewed and reinforced to meet this changed situation. Effective early warning and preventive action must be at the core of maintaining international peace and security. The United Nations will have to devise rapid-response mechanisms. The setting up of UN "peace enforcement units," proposed in the *Agenda for Peace*, could be one such measure. For refugee-related emergencies, UNHCR has installed five "emergency preparedness and response teams" for rapid deployment of staff and goods. For various crises in other realms – natural disaster, nuclear calamity, financial market crash, etc. – effective countervailing measures will have to be installed because emergency in one realm tends to trigger emergency in others. Together with early warning and rapid emergency response capacity, legal principles and effective mechanisms must be developed that recognize the evolving nature of state sovereignty and expanding international responsibility.

Since the early 1900s, humanitarian crises have come to the forefront of public attention. In the course of this lecture, I have tried to elaborate on some of the emerging trends towards linking humanitarian and political activities. At the same time, I have as yet to recognize any clear mode of adjustment or agreed division of labour between the two realms. The challenge for crisis management in today's world is to devise a system that balances the state's concern for territorial integrity with the protection needs of minorities and individuals while effectively meeting the multiple nature of threats that affect both states and peoples. Such a system cannot be developed only by political leaders and decision-makers since it involves the protection and well-being of individuals and peoples. Greater mobilization of the wisdom and efforts of peoples from all walks of life – human rights specialists, humanitarian workers, NGOs – all are needed. Particularly, greater contributions are expected from the academic and research community, as well as the thinking public at large to build an international system that gives full allowance to the humanitarian needs.

May 1993

The Future of Europe
Managing Economic and Social Change

JACQUES DELORS

It is a great pleasure to contribute to this volume under the auspices of the Sylvia Ostry Foundation. Sylvia Ostry's contribution to our understanding of international economic issues is recognized not only in university circles but also among governments and policy-makers. She has enlightened us through her perspectives on the economic data and has helped us to see problems in a new light.

The adventure of building the new Europe is not at all, as you know, like a long, tranquil river – to borrow the title of a French film. However, progress is being made, even though it is constantly threatened by the challenges of the future and the very worrisome re-emergence in Europe of ideologies that advocate non-recognition and rejection of all that is different. For this reason, although I intend the concentrate on economic and social change in Europe, trying to explain our current difficulties, I feel obliged to mention another major concern of today's European Union, namely security. Security in Europe, in the broad sense, but also security throughout the world, because Europe cannot deal with all the areas around it, whether to the east or to the north. After dealing at length with economic and social questions, I will say a few words about security concerns and the obligations that are incumbent, I believe, on the European Union and, more generally, on the generations that have now risen to positions of influence.

After several years of strong growth between 1985 and 1990 (due, I like to think, to the target date of 1992 and its promise of a vast market free of internal borders), Europe is now passing through a recession, like other countries such as Canada's or the United States. It is a deep recession, which prompts us to pose a few questions about the changes underway in Europe. Is mass unemployment and reduced competitiveness a sign of the European disease? Or is this a disease of developed industrial societies in general? Perhaps the difficulties stem from the mounting globalization of the economy and worldwide problems. So what are the questions we are now asking that will help us re-consider macroeconomic policies, labour market policies, and education policies? This leads to an even more fundamental question: Are we not in the process of going through a radical change in the world we have inhabited since the end of the world war?

First the European disease. As I said, 1985 to 1990 was a time when there was no more talk of Euro-sclerosis, especially in the United States, but rather of Euro-optimism. Concerns were arising about what was called "Fortress Europe," although in fact we are the largest trading power in the world and have therefore a market that is more open than many people think. During these years, Europe changed. The construction of Europe gained renewed credibility. We created nine million new jobs between 1985 and 1990, whereas we had lost two and a half million during the previous five years. Our growth rate doubled and, most of all, investment increased, with the result that our economies were modernized – insufficiently, of course, but real progress was made.

After these steps in the right direction, however, we suffered the recession that was spreading throughout the industrialized countries. I say the "industrialized countries" and not the world because, during this period, the countries of Asia and the Pacific experienced and are still experiencing remarkable economic growth. The recession we suffered was all the deeper because the effects of what was happening in the dominant economy of the United States were magnified, shortly thereafter, by the negative consequences of German unification. At that point, doubts resurfaced and some observers claimed that the European miracle was finished. So what is the outlook? Three questions arise: How can we enhance our competitiveness? How can we enhance the correlation between growth and employment? – for the results in Europe have been much weaker than the results in the United States for similar growth rates. How, finally, can we greatly improve all policies that affect employment?

These questions are tackled in the White Paper I submitted to the Council of Europe in order to provide the twelve member countries with an outline for both joint action and, most importantly, debate in each country necessitated to take into account the diversity of their situations, especially in regard to employment systems.

First, how can we enhance our competitiveness? Our efforts in the area of research are insufficient in view of the rapidity and extent of the changes brought about by progress in science and technology. Even though we have our strong points, particularly in pharmaceuticals, the food industry, chemicals, and everything related to biotechnology, as well as to telecommunications, we certainly have lost a great many battles. I shall not enumerate them all here.

We do not have enough research because our investment rates are too low, even though our savings rates are satisfactory. According to our forecasts, our investment rates would have to rise from 20 to 25 per cent of gross national product in order for us to feel assured that we are laying solid foundations for the future. We do have some comparative advantages. Our human capital, as we saw at the Detroit conference organized in the framework of the G7, is better trained than that in other countries. Our savings and financial services are efficient. The common market forms the strategic foundation for our companies. This market of 350 million consumers, under the 1992 target, has created a base for our companies (if we were speaking in military terms) from which they can strike out on what must now be, for big business, a worldwide level. Ultimately, though, we need to enhance our research efforts, both qualitatively and quantitatively, and invest more.

Second, how can we improve the correlation between growth and employment? In this regard, I mentioned an interesting parallel between the European Union and the United States, where President Clinton is concerned about the creation of marginal jobs, which he calls "work pools," that do not enable the people who hold them to meet their basic needs, in view of the social system in the United States. You could say, therefore, that Europe is too rigid, although the educational system is good, while the United States is more flexible but has an apparently unsatisfactory educational system. We need to study the relationship between growth and employment, without, however, accepting a decline in productivity, especially in the area of services, that would undermine the macroeconomic competitiveness of the European economies. From this point of view, our efforts should focus on two points: first, sharing the added value, and second, seeking out new kinds of employment.

First, sharing the added value. In Europe over the past twenty years, we did not really understand the warning sent out by the first oil shock. Those who had jobs and those who provided them, in other words employees and employers, discussed the distribution of the added value or increases in productivity without much concern for those who had no jobs. This is quite clear. We have calculated that if you want to cut the unemployment rate in Europe by half, reduce it from 11 per cent to 5.5 or 6 per cent by the end of the century, you would have to devote all the increases in productivity over the next five years to job creation and investment alone. This is inescapable if you want to reverse the trends in employment.

Second, we have to find new kinds of employment. There is no shortage of work to be done, and it is therefore rather curious to see some people in Europe developing a Malthusian attitude that presupposes, without ever quite saying, that there is a fixed quantity of work to do and it should therefore be distributed among a larger group of people, i.e., not only among the 90 per cent who have jobs but among all 100 per cent. I have not resigned myself to this approach – even though I believe (and I will return to this later) that technical progress results in a progressive reduction in the hours of work.

In any case, re-distribution of work is not the miracle cure for the unemployment problem in Europe. We need to look, therefore, for new kinds of work. Ultimately I think of an observation made by Lord Keynes in 1930. He said at the time that technical progress outpaces our ability to imagine new needs. However, because he was an optimist, he said that living standards would rise by three or four times and new needs would develop to be satisfied. Today as well, a gap has opened between rapid technical progress and our ability to imagine new needs that would generate new jobs.

The third question that we are asking in Europe is how to radically improve our employment systems. By "employment systems" I mean the entire nexus of education and training policies, the organization of work in business, the management of internal employment markets within companies, external labour markets, and the social assistance programs that underlie the labour market.

These employment systems worked well in Europe, particularly in Sweden, but were then swamped by unemployment. In other words, a point was reached where the number of people to be helped made it impossible to preserve the priorities we had set. The dramatic increase in unemployment swamped even the best systems. Nowadays, apart from Sweden and also Denmark, we have an employment system whose implicit priority is compensating the unemployed. Its lowest priority is passionately seeking out jobs, activities, or training for the unemployed or for young people arriving on the labour market.

This trend must be reversed. Nowadays, the priority of the employment systems – I might say the passionate priority – must be to find employment, some kind of activity (because some activity is better than simple unemployment) or training that enables people to recover their self-confidence and find a job. It should be a blend of professional knowledge, that has to be up-to-date, and concrete know-how that enables people to assume productive jobs.

Every country must therefore make a great effort and, thanks to the White Paper, most European countries are now holding seminars, meetings, and discussions among public authorities, employer organizations, and unions to consider these facts. They need to make it a priority to provide jobs, activities, or training and to provide the employment services with the means that are needed, both qualitative and quantitative. In addition, they need to make labour markets more flexible, not only external markets but also internal markets within companies because European businesses have recently tended to overemphasize the role of their labour forces as a variable that can be adjusted.

If we calculate in terms of capital, and not simply in terms of gross national product, we would see that we have overlooked potential wealth and that we have made cost-benefit analyses that were not necessarily as good as they could be. Reducing the cost of unskilled labour is absolutely essential. Workers with few skills cost too much in Europe. Why? Because in ten of the twelve countries in the European Union the social security system is 80 per cent financed by levies on wages. Since there can be no question of reducing low wages – that would be contrary to providing minimum support for demand – it is the financing of the social security system that is called into question. The European Commission has made a proposal in this regard, which some consider revolutionary, that is based on a simple principle:

labour has become an abundant, highly available commodity in Europe. It is heavily taxed. Depending on the country, you have to add between 50 and 70 per cent to wages in order to obtain the real cost of labour. On the other hand, there are no taxes at all on the declining environment. We have therefore suggested a trade: taxes on labour should be eliminated, while taxes should be imposed on everything that pollutes our national capital – hence the tax on carbon dioxide. This has given rise to strenuous debate, but I think we will succeed in the end and will manage to shift 1 or 2 per cent, a not insignificant amount, of our gross national product.

Finally, a fourth element in these thoughts about the employment system: we need to emphasize life-long education and training. I myself tabled a bill on continuing education in France in 1971, and when you look at the results, you could say either that the glass is half empty or half full. We could do much better in this area. In other words, the universe of the mass media, which now envelops us and our young people, the rapidity of change, the structural reorganizations of the economy, and the extent of technical progress all lead us, even force us, to re-educate ourselves throughout our lives. In order to understand all these changes, you have to be educated in addition to having job training. These, then, are the avenues that Europe is exploring, without worrying too much about the problems of others, in an attempt to reverse a dramatic turn of events, particularly in regard to unemployment and the long-term unemployment that affects nearly half of all the unemployed.

However, we must also ask ourselves another question. Is this not a problem that is inherent in all industrial societies? This question, in fact, was at the heart of the Detroit conference. You could say of industrial societies, and even of Japan nowadays, that, looking beyond the statistics, "they were not all withering away but they were all affected" by this lack of job creation. Beyond our own particular weaknesses – and I pointed out Europe's – what if we are witnessing a radical change in our world, as I suggested in my introduction? A change caused by the globalization of problems, technical progress, and shifting values and behaviours. In the Commission's White Paper, we advance some hypotheses about these changes and point out some methods of attempting to prepare for them: the information highway, for instance, which will make information a more valuable commodity than the goods and services that we produce; time management; and many others.

However, all these questions, including those concerning the labour market, should not distract from the most basic question. Where do we find the demand to stimulate growth, even though this growth could never be sufficient? This was one of the topics of the debate at Detroit, although it was a bit fuzzy and elusive, between those who emphasize monetary stability, somewhat excessively in my view, and those who want at least the industrialized countries, as a whole, in other words 900 million out of a total of 5.5 billion people, to arrange among themselves to create the necessary conditions for economic growth. I cannot, however, discuss at this point economic growth, macroeconomic policy per se, or various priorities at a given point in time.

The educational and information system: We must prepare and design the educational system for the day when virtually no jobs exist solely to produce goods and services – they must expand knowledge as well.

Finally, I think we must consider as well the place of work in society. As I mentioned earlier, technical progress has reduced the hours of work, and this will continue. Someone who is lucky enough to work in Europe devotes, I believe, about 70,000 hours of his or her lifetime to it. Without much chance of going far wrong, we can imagine that in twenty years this number will fall to only 40,000 hours. This is an enormous change that we have to begin thinking about now. I spoke a little while ago about the commodity called information. Time itself will become a key commodity. And how will this time be occupied? Will our cities, our leisure activities, make this possible? Will we escape the classic cycle that we have gone through since the beginning of industrialized society: we study until the age of sixteen, twenty, or maybe twenty-five, then we work, and then, after the age of sixty or sixty-five, we live off the accumulated product of our labours.

This cycle is called into question, I believe, by contemporary society, first of all because education no longer ceases. You need continual education throughout your life. Second, our early retirement systems waste a large amount of capital in the form of experience. I was greatly saddened to see, in a number of countries, fifty-year-old men and women retiring when they were still capable not only of working but of bringing their wealth of experience to bear. All this is no longer appropriate, I believe, in a society where people will only work for 40,000 hours in their lifetimes. We will have to organize things differently and invent life cycles that are more appropriate.

These are the changes that are underway. We can either succumb to them or control them. A new society will emerge as a result of what we do. Beyond the immediate concerns of our governments, their short-term problems, and the polls that sadden or delight them, the Commission's White Paper was intended to open a window on the mid-term, to raise their gaze a little further. As an eminent futurologist, Gaston Berger, once said: "To look into the future is to begin changing already."

Third, and finally, are the problems related to globalization. New competitors are obviously emerging. We can no longer speak, as we used to, about relations between North and South; now it is between the North and Souths. The countries of Asia and the Pacific are experiencing rapid development. The renewal of democracy in Latin America has brought undeniable economic progress as well, even though serious social inequities remain. Finally there is Africa, which, according to the stock phrase that I hope will soon become antiquated, remains the "forgotten continent" of development.

There are, of course, people in Europe who think it is unacceptable that outsiders should take not only market share but also jobs. I have calculated that since the early 1970s, in the open market that Europe has become, five million jobs have had to be eliminated, particularly in industry, in order for us to maintain our standard of living and our social welfare system. There is therefore a connection between globalization and our employment situation.

To be frank, though, should we really complain that new countries are beginning to develop economically when we have been asking people to feel sorry about poverty in the Third World for the past thirty years? What hypocrisy! I myself am happy that these countries are growing and developing. If we have to increase the length of the dinner table, let's do it and deal with the consequences.

What actually happened in the nineteenth century? At the beginning of the industrial era, some people grew rich while others were impoverished or remained poor. No one bothered to count the unemployed at this time, but there were certainly more than there are now. Then we found methods of spreading the wealth and creating employment. This is what experts in social economics call "Fordism." Why don't we start practising Fordism on a world scale, enabling these countries to develop and thereby to increase the living standards of their billions of people, while allowing us to produce for new needs? Here as well, I think that adopting a Malthusian view would be to turn our backs on the future.

Rules of the game are needed, of course, and in this regard we can salute, now that the event has finally happened, the signature of the Uruguay Round of the World Trade Organization negotiations by 109 countries. It is to be hoped, and it is indeed my hope, that the WTO being created will succeed in establishing more equitable rules of the game and introducing some viewpoints other than commerce pure and simple, such as the environment, social considerations, and even the play of currency values. All this is still open. Finally, we should be delighted that after much difficult thought we succeeded in developing some rules of the game. We should be pleased with the results of the Uruguay Round of 109 countries that approved very large reductions in tariffs, the extension of freedom of movement to services, and many other positive elements. Here too, however, we should not look for miracle solutions. The Uruguay Round is not going to immediately restore prosperity to our countries. Nevertheless, it is a sign that a world economy is emerging that may be able to manage its interdependence – something that is not the case in 1994.

For we Europeans, this is a major concern because the vast majority of us want to preserve the kind of societies we have. Our social model is predicated on two simple principles: first, a social protection system for all, and second, a market-based economy, which is accompanied by the recognition that certain responsibilities are incumbent upon public institutions, such as governments and central banks, and by a social dialogue among employers, unions, and, sometimes, public authorities. For years, right-wing ideologues have been condemning this model. And yet, in April 1994, a newspaper that generally disparages the European social model had to admit that the Federal Republic of Germany, one of the prototypes of this model, was in the process of radically altering its economy and improving its structures while preserving its social model, which is an example of the European model.

Of course, maintaining our social security systems does not mean preserving them exactly as they are. They have to be adapted, for they are developing holes. How can you say that our social security systems are universal when we have 30 million poor in the European Union? Something needs to be done. This is particularly true of some payments and some excessive costs in the area of health. The duty of politicians and officials is to explain to Europeans the conditions under which they can save their social model. These conditions are a refusal of Malthusianism and a willingness to embrace technical progress, openness to others, and a sense of international solidarity. Without this, Europe will soon be on the sidelines.

As I mentioned earlier, Europe also has security concerns. This is a paradox of the post–Cold War. The Cold War provided, to some extent, the peace of the graveyard. Since the collapse of Communism, however, the danger of conflict, unrest, and instability has escalated, not just in Europe, but especially there. This is the tragic side of history. The people who built the new Europe, who conceived it, the fathers of the Treaty of Rome, if they were still with us, would certainly expect us to rise to meet this new challenge. Are we going to accept the re-emergence of ideologies, the rejection of those who are different, populism, racism, even religious wars, as can be seen in part of the former Yugoslavia? Or are we going to succeed in extending our values of peace to all of greater Europe? Finally, beyond greater Europe – since it is the fiftieth anniversary of the United Nations – how can rules be developed at the global level that enable us to meet the needs of a world that is in the process of unifying?

We try to ensure security, first, through economic cooperation. Contrary to what is often claimed – not so much in Canada but in the United States – we have largely opened our markets to the new countries of Central and Eastern Europe. Our imports from these countries have doubled in four years, while American imports have remained virtually unchanged. The same is true for the countries of the Mediterranean and Africa. We know that it is much better to buy from these countries than to make loans to them, even though there is a large portion of financial assistance in our efforts. The European Union also provides two-thirds of the assistance to the countries of the former Soviet Union and to the countries of Central and Eastern Europe in the form of technical assistance, subsidies, and loans. It is interesting to note, for example, that as a financial institution we have done as much for these countries over the last four years as the International Monetary Fund.

However, there are readily apparent limitations influencing affairs through economic means. The best illustration of this is the Yugoslav tragedy, although there are also dangers that the Balkans will see the re-emergence of the fears and antipathies of the past. We can see this as well among our neighbours to the south, with the spread of religious fundamentalism. In short, it is impossible to believe that the European Union can assume its responsibilities and extend security in Europe solely through economic means. For this reason, our agenda includes the construction of greater Europe. This is not an agenda for a few years hence but for right now. As I said before, this is a duty incumbent upon our generations. I would remind you of the dual purpose that motivated the fathers of the united Europe, whose direct heirs we are. The first was to promulgate the values of peace, cooperation, and mutual recognition through a simple formula that helped to get a united Europe started: "Never again war among us." The second was to get our countries to join their strengths because none of them alone, even if it had been a great power in the past, was capable of playing the same role today.

So these are our two objectives. The first reflects a belief in cooperation and the second a belief in a political Europe. This gives rise to the duty incumbent upon our generations to extend these values to the rest of Europe, while creating the political instrument that these countries need if they want to progress. This, then, is the great debate now beginning in Europe between those who want to see the construction of a greater Europe and those who prefer first to strengthen the political Europe. Unfortunately, I believe, we have to do both, even though they contradict one another – institutionally, economically, and politically. In order to do this, we have to move very quickly from cooperation to political partnership.

The countries of Central and Eastern Europe should be offered, in my opinion at least, a plan for political cooperation that would guarantee their security. Some attempts have been made, such as

Partnership for Peace, but they do not feel that this is sufficient. The French have proposed the idea of a stability pact in Europe. Many institutions would be involved and it is difficult to see how it would work, but the basic idea is there. The countries involved – whether Poland, the Czech Republic, Hungary, Slovakia, Slovenia, Bulgaria, Romania, or the Baltic states – must feel that they are out of danger thanks to a cooperation accord with the European Union. In addition, those who might be tempted to destabilize these countries, from within or without, must be dissuaded. This, of course, is not easy to do, especially since Russia is wary of such efforts. Therefore, at the same time that we offer these countries an agreement for political cooperation, we should establish a political partnership with Russia. Russia cannot join the European Union – it is so huge that we would never recover from the resulting destabilization. At the very least, however, we should establish a political partnership that recognizes Russia as a great power, despite its economic and perhaps, unfortunately, political problems, and that makes it possible to live on our continent in an atmosphere of cooperation, while the countries of Central and Eastern Europe are assured of their security.

With regard to our neighbours to the south, we should initiate an overall Mediterranean policy, although a successful conclusion to such a policy is made very difficult by events, in Algeria in particular. What we are trying, or at least what I propose to do for Europe, could be extended *mutatis mutandis* to the entire world. In view of the globalization of problems, the interdependence of activities, and a worldwide economy, there is a need – if you will allow me to utter the words – for a fledgling world government. The Rio conference was very significant in this regard. Everybody realizes that the environment has no frontiers and that we must therefore cooperate in creating a master plan to bequeath to our children a natural capital that is still in good shape. We do not, however, have the institutions to do this. I used the environment as an example, but I could also have mentioned currencies. In the strictly political and military sphere, the United Nations is increasingly asked to help out. Its secretary-general told me that in the past five years it has had to intervene as often as it did in the previous forty years. The UN appears to be absolutely essential, but it is also hobbled by its decision-making process and a lack of action. We need to consider all this.

For my part, I think action should be taken in two areas. First, the UN Charter should be modified, especially chapters 6 and 7, in regard to the right of intervention discussed here. What should the decision-making process be (one can see with regard to events in the former Yugoslavia how difficult it is to make decisions that satisfy everyone) and what methods should be used? These questions alone deserve an entire speech. I would like, though, just to mention them because there is a double confusion in the public mind. First, humanitarian intervention and political intervention are confused. This goes so far that some politicians achieve great success by encouraging confusion of the two and acting as if humanitarian intervention could solve political problems. As if things were that easy! The second source of confusion is the fact that the public sees all these dramas unfold on television but they are quickly forgotten. Tragedy is now consumed as goods and services used to be.

The second area to which we should devote some thought is the creation of an Economic Security Council. Why? Because the action by international organizations is now scattered among the International Monetary Fund, the World Bank, the United Nations Educational, Scientific, and Cultural Organization (UNESCO), the International Labour Organization, and the World Trade Organization. When the leaders of the industrialized countries have their G7 meetings (since I take part in these I cannot be accused of unstinting negativism), they are covered by 2,000 or 3,000 journalists, even though the results are not very important. However, only 900 million people live in the industrialized countries, out of a total of 5.5 billion on the planet. For these reasons, I think we need an Economic Security Council made up of the great powers (whether in economic or demographic terms) as well as the presidents of geographic organizations. They would meet two or three times a year and these meetings would help raise the consciousness of the world about the great vertically integrated international organizations. This would not immediately resolve all our problems, of course. It would help, however, to promulgate a general awareness of our interdependence and of the absolute necessity, sooner or later, of creating new institutions and new methods of resolving our problems in order to prevent economic difficulties from sparking a new protectionism or even future conflict. In other words, what I would like to see is the birth of an international consciousness that reflects the realities of today's world.

Mass unemployment is not inevitable. However, if we fail to find solutions in the near future, the European social model will disappear and we will live in a three-speed society: those who have secure, guaranteed jobs; those who have marginal jobs; and those who have no chance of finding employment. Even today there are young people at university in Europe who have never seen either their father or mother hold down a job. All this threatens to destabilize our society.

The reasons we carry on the struggle in Europe (never again war among us and the values of peace that gave birth to the new Europe) have not changed. They are a moral imperative for the generations that have now assumed positions of responsibility. Avoiding responsibility for our problems will only mean that they will come crashing down on those who are now in their twenties or thirties.

Finally, the clear trend to globalization and worldwide problems is not incompatible with the formation of regional groupings such as the European Union or the North American Free Trade Agreement (NAFTA). Some people have decried these kinds of organizations, claiming that they fragment the world. I do not share this view. Regional institutions provide a means for better understanding the world, for getting a handle on it and managing its interdependence, in a more limited way at first, to be sure, but then more globally. All in all, there is no reason to despair about humankind's intelligence or ability to innovate.

April 1994

The International Monetary Fund in a Globalized World Economy
The Tasks Ahead

MICHEL CAMDESSUS

It is a great pleasure and a privilege for me to have this opportunity to pay tribute to Sylvia Ostry and to do so in Canada, a country with such a tradition of openness to international cooperation and held in very high respect in all international fora. For more than fifteen years I have had the honour of counting Sylvia as a friend and ally in many a battle for international economic cooperation. In Paris in the early 1980s I witnessed at first hand the intellectual leadership she provided as head of the Economics Department of the Organization for Economic Cooperation and Development (OECD) during one of the deepest recessions of the postwar period; and I saw the energy she applied to focusing the work of the OECD on the supply side and structural reforms – an orientation that still holds good. Shortly after she returned home to Canada in 1984, she was named Ambassador for Multilateral Trade Negotiations, and we all know the vital role she played in the Uruguay Round discussions. She was among the few who saw clearly and early on that fundamental institutional reform – the creation of a World Trade Organization – had become indispensable. The World Trade Organization (WTO) was finally established at the beginning of 1995, completing at long last the three-pillared institutional structure for the promotion of international monetary cooperation, development, and trade – the International Monetary Fund (IMF), the World Bank, and the WTO – envisaged by our founding fathers at Bretton Woods more than fifty years ago.

This early period is well described in Sir Nicholas Bayne's book *Hanging Together*, but let me recall some landmarks, culled from the compendium of communiqués from successful summits. From Bonn in 1985, when protectionism was looming ominously, I can cite the statement that "open multilateral trade is essential to global prosperity," which presaged the launching of the Uruguay Round in the following year. In Tokyo of 1986, coming just after the Plaza Agreement, the G7 decided that their finance ministers would subsequently meet regularly between summits and agreed to "close and continuous coordination" of economic policies and to cooperation with the IMF to strengthen multilateral surveillance. In Venice in 1987, the heads of state and government endorsed the Louvre Accord to foster exchange-rate stability and acknowledged that international policy coordination "is essential to achieving stronger and sustained global growth, reduced external imbalances, and more stable exchange-rate relationships." The Venice Summit also endorsed my proposal for an enhanced structural adjustment facility (ESAF) at the IMF to meet the needs of low-income countries. Eight years later, I can tell you that ESAF arrangements have made it possible to introduce growth-oriented programs of adjustment and reform in thirty-seven of the poorest countries in the world and that these programs have succeeded beyond most expectations. Finally, the 1988 Toronto Summit is justly renowned for developing the "Toronto terms" that provided the basis for official debt relief agreements over the following years – just one example of Canadian leadership on behalf of the poorest.

I remain convinced that there is a common good for the international community that it is time to identify and promote; that, as Sir Nicholas pointed out in 1984, few remarks are more applicable to summits than what Benjamin Franklin said upon signing the Declaration of Independence, "We must indeed all hang together or most assuredly, we shall all hang separately";[1] and, finally, that in these times of what Sylvia Ostry has aptly termed "techno-nationalism" and "techno-globalism," there are certain subjects on which it is essential that the common voice of heads of state and government be heard.

Given this I would like to discuss the Halifax Summit, the subjects I would like to see raised there, and, in passing, to make a few suggestions about what tasks should lie ahead for the IMF in this globalized world economy.

⁂

Let us examine first a number of features that are peculiar to this twenty-first summit of the industrial countries. The first is that its agenda, if rumour is to be trusted, grew out of the desires and vision of the heads of state and governments themselves. It is the leaders, not the techno-structure, who asked the two major questions set forth in the preamble to the Naples Summit of the G-7 Group, namely: "(1) How can we assure that the global economy of the twenty-first century will provide sustainable development with good prosperity and well-being of the peoples of our nations and the world? (2) What framework of institutions will be required to meet these challenges in the twenty-first century? How can we adapt existing institutions and build new institutions to ensure the future prosperity and security of our people?" It is fortunate that these questions were chosen and, six months after

1 R.D. Putnam and Nicholas Bayne, *Hanging Together: The Seven-Power Summits* (London: Heinemann for the Royal Institute of International Affairs, 1984)

the Naples Summit, three major monetary and financial crises have confirmed how appropriate this agenda is.

Everything is happening as if, in the first half of 1995, we had already embarked on the twenty-first century, making this twenty-first summit, in effect, the first summit of the twenty-first century. But judge for yourselves: Mexico, Barings, the dollar crisis. These three crises bear the marks of a new world dominated by the forces of globalization, a world to which our countries and our institutions are urgently required to adapt as well as they can. It is against this background that the Halifax Summit will take place.

Finally, the third feature of this summit is that because the globalization process is also characterized by the emergence of many countries that now play or are preparing to play major roles in the international financial arena, it is important that at this meeting the G7 countries make clear their intention to give these new partners the role they deserve in the management of the world economy.

Having said this, one conclusion is inescapable: Halifax is already a summit of the twenty-first century, dealing with the next century's challenges. And what subjects might be raised there to address them? Of course, first, there are the issues that should already have been resolved, the ever-present issues of the first twenty summits; second, there are the urgent questions necessarily raised by these new crises of the twenty-first century.

The challenges we face in the world economy in 1995 are in many respects remarkably similar to those encountered in the mid-1980s. First, even though the Uruguay Round negotiations are now behind us and the World Trade Organization (WTO) is in place, there is no room for complacency on trade relations. Protectionism, unilateralism, and associated trade frictions are still with us. Ostry and Nelson[2] discuss the benefits of a transparent,

2 Sylvia Ostry and R.R. Nelson, *Techno-nationalism and Techno-globalism: Conflict and Cooperation* (Washington, D.C.: The Brookings Institution, 1995).

rules-based multilateral trade system in terms of predictability, stability, and restraint on the use of trade policy to achieve political objectives. They go on to say that "The loss of these international public goods in an increasingly interdependent world would be serious in the extreme." At present, there is one serious bilateral dispute that exemplifies these dangers. We must clearly be wary of assuming that strengthened multilateral trade rules by themselves will keep unilateral action at bay, or make the protectionist threat disappear. Strong political will is also required to ensure that trade frictions are resolved within the framework of the multilateral trade rules overseen by the WTO. I hope that this wish will be heard, and that such tensions will not divert the attention of the Summit from its primary aims. I know that we can rely on Prime Minister Chrétien to avert this, and to ensure that this summit gives the WTO the firm backing it requires at its inception.

The second familiar issue is the intensification of our efforts in favour of the developing countries, many of whom have made great progress since the mid-1980s, thanks in part to adjustment and reform programs supported by the International Monetary Fund (IMF) and the World Bank. Their dynamism has contributed markedly to continuing global growth in recent years, despite the slowdown in the industrial countries. Many others, however, especially in Africa, are still mired in poverty. What is more, while globalization is a monumental force of economic integration that can benefit the poor countries by speeding their development, it may also lead to the marginalization of those countries that refuse to undertake, or are prevented from undertaking, the necessary structural adjustment effort.

While the overall strategy for the poor countries has been well established for some time, two of its components are of major importance and call for particular attention from the Seven. One is the World Bank's concessional loan facility, the International Development Agency (IDA). Let us not mince words – for the poorest countries that have resolved to do everything in their power to get out of their difficulties, there is no credible solution in the absence of IDA-type resources in sufficient volume at the World Bank. Without a sizable replenishment of IDA resources, a critical component of the development strategy would be lacking, particularly for Africa. The IMF's efforts to put in place the macroeconomic preconditions for growth, through its enhanced structural adjustment facility, would be in vain. Such an IDA replenishment is therefore a major priority, along with our efforts to ensure that the ESAF remains operational after the resources provided by its first replenishment have been drawn down. We now know that the problem of the poorest countries is one that will be with us well into the next century. If we seek to address it credibly, and if, as the chancellor of the exchequer suggests, we wish to be in a position to deal with the problem of the countries most heavily indebted to the multilateral institutions, continuing the ESAF is essential. Indeed, I would propose that the IMF contribute itself by using its own resources – including, if necessary, limited amounts of gold – provided that this is done, I hasten to stress, in concert with a commensurate effort by bilateral donors.

The third challenge is progress in the transitional economies. In Naples, the G7 reminded us that the Bretton Woods institutions were founded on two major principles: democracy and open markets. Nowhere has our work been guided more by these two beacons than in our efforts to promote the successful transformation of the former centrally planned economies. In 1995 more than half of the economies in transition in Eastern Europe and the former Soviet Union have recently begun to experience growth after several years of stagnation or decline. While this development is significant, our efforts must continue; it is essential that the countries that have progressed the least on the transformation path know that the G7 is resolved to support them, just as they did in the early, euphoric first years following the fall of the Berlin Wall.

It is well known that the international financial institutions are continuing and intensifying their efforts, but all too often inadequate levels of bilateral support cause the postponement of financing programs or a reduction in the volume of imports, however essential they may be. It is my fervent hope that decisions will be reached on bilateral contributions and debt restructuring in amounts that will dispel despair. Finally, as soon as possible, these countries should be given all the prerogatives of our membership; in this regard, the time has come to move forward, as indicated by the Naples Summit, to an allocation of Special Drawing Rights that will place the transition countries and all other new members on a par with our members of longer standing.

There is finally a fourth theme, which, in this more and more globalized world, takes on added importance – market stabilization. This is a matter of renewed and deep concern, since the increasing international integration of markets, and especially the globalization of financial markets, mean that international financial flows at times have a frightening dimension that makes the calls for their stabilization more pressing. Let me refer to just a few examples. The outstanding amount of international bond issues rose to above US$2 trillion in 1994 from less than US$600 billion in 1985; over the same period international bank loans tripled to US$4 trillion. Cross-border securities transactions in most industrial countries, including Canada, expanded to well above 100 per cent of GDP in 1992 from less than 10 per cent at the beginning of the 1980s. Trading in foreign exchange markets has accelerated in tandem with international securities transactions: estimates put current turnover at around US$1 trillion a day, roughly a four-fold increase from a decade ago.

The globalization of financial markets has brought great benefits by fostering a more efficient allocation of global savings and boosting investment and growth in many countries. But to preserve these benefits, we must face up to the downside: vastly increased financial flows across national borders have also made countries that participate in international financial markets more vulnerable both to excessively favourable and to adverse shifts in market sentiment. And the adverse shifts, though generally related to concerns about economic fundamentals and policy shortcomings, can often be delayed, sudden, massive, and destabilizing. So financial globalization has heightened the challenges of fostering stable foreign exchange and financial markets, and of preventing and resolving financial crises. This carries important implications both for economic policies in all countries and for the IMF as the central institution of the international monetary system. Let us see how to handle this difficult new part of our agenda.

EXCHANGE MARKET STABILIZATION

This has been a constant item on the agenda of the summits since the beginning, as is appropriate for meetings of the countries responsible for the key reserve currencies of the world. I will not reopen the old debate between those who believe that the best way to achieve a reasonable degree of exchange rate stability is to rely essentially on the pursuit of domestic macroeconomic stability together with effective policy coordination among the major countries, and those – among whom I would count myself – who believe that the adoption of a more rules-based system of exchange rate stabilization could add to the efficiency of the whole endeavour. It is clear, in the present circumstances, that only the first approach has enough support. But there is no doubt that significant progress can be made toward stability if the major countries take seriously their macroeconomic responsibilities and their special responsibilities as issuers of reserve currencies. More than other countries, they have to recognize that "the foreign exchange markets," as German Finance Minister Theo Waigel says, are "exceedingly sensitive to even the smallest credibility gap in monetary as in fiscal policy." The IMF has a role to play in helping the G7 countries in this process through its particular regime of oversight, or surveillance. Several suggestions have been made to strengthen Fund surveillance, some, some time ago by Wendy Dobson, and some in June 1995 by Morris Goldstein. We stand ready to do our best, knowing how important it could be for the world to contribute to exemplary behaviour by the G7 in this field.

STRENGTHENING SURVEILLANCE AND CRISIS PREVENTION

The other aspect of our surveillance work deals with the financial markets overall and relates to the prevention and cure of major financial crises, of which Mexico has been a telling example. Openness to the world economy and international financial markets – an essential ingredient in Mexico's success in the late 1980s and early 1990s – today imposes an obligation of unfailing discipline on economic policy. Vigilance and discipline provide the most effective deterrent and defence against financial market setbacks. Mexico, unfortunately, after remarkable progress on many macro and structural fronts, had lowered its guard. As a result, the markets eventually exercised their own discipline, and Mexico paid a very high cost in the process.

But what does the globalized world economy require of the IMF? Essentially two things: the Fund can help countries – and help them more effectively – to improve their policies, so that currency misalignments and balance of payments crises are less likely to occur; and it can provide financial support for corrective policy action when crises do occur. In both areas, the Fund is seeking to ensure that it is strong enough to serve its purposes in the new environment of globalized markets, and I hope that the G7 will endorse, encourage, and help to speed up the steps we are taking or planning to take.

The IMF's work in promoting exchange market stability and preventing crises is carried out mainly through the exercise of its responsibility for surveillance over the international monetary system and countries' exchange rate policies. Fund surveillance is an international cooperative effort aimed at improvements in policies, and it should work as an early warning system, alerting governments to policies that need correction, and enabling them to encourage each other to take necessary measures. Over a number of years, with the encouragement of the membership – the Tokyo Summit Declaration, for example, which I referred to earlier – the Fund has taken action to make surveillance more effective, and significant progress has been made. Fund surveillance has achieved many successes, although these have tended to go unnoticed: crises prevented are usually crises unseen.

Mexico's crisis showed that further adaptations are needed to make surveillance sufficiently strong to minimize the risk of the eruption and spread of crises in the new global environment:

- first, data: stricter requirements need to be applied concerning the regular and timely communication by countries to the IMF of data on key economic indicators, and the Fund also needs to make more use of financial market data in monitoring developments. We shall also be working toward the establishment of standards for the timely publication of economic data by members to help markets work more efficiently;
- second, closer and more continuous policy dialogue: not only must countries be willing to keep the IMF informed of developments and seek its opinion on issues they are facing but the Fund's internal procedures must be adapted to foster dialogue more effectively in the intervals between regular consultations, particularly when countries have just ended an adjustment program with the Fund;
- third, better focused surveillance: especially given its limited resources, the Fund must focus more effectively on countries at risk, and countries where financial tensions are most likely to

have spillover effects. And surveillance must also focus more carefully on international financial flows and their sustainability.
- fourth, more pointed and candid surveillance: in its policy dialogue with member countries the Fund must be prepared to be more critical and demanding – even more critical and demanding than in the past.

These are the main items on our agenda of action to strengthen surveillance. It was endorsed at the ministerial level by the Interim Committee in April 1995. I fear that implementing it will not be a straightforward matter: experience shows that while countries tend to be very eager for surveillance over others, they are less keen on surveillance over themselves. It will be a critical challenge for international policy cooperation and for the IMF. It is therefore important that the leaders of the G7 re-affirm their commitment to it.

THE RESOLUTION OF CRISES

But even the most effective IMF surveillance would not eliminate financial crises altogether; and the IMF must also ensure that it has the means to provide countries with financial assistance adequate to contribute effectively to the resolution of crises when they occur. It was able to do so in the case of Mexico, by virtue of the increase in IMF quotas, supported by Canada, that came into effect in 1992, and by applying the rules allowing the Fund in exceptional circumstances to exceed the limits that apply to the use of its credit. The Fund's commitment to Mexico is the largest in the Fund's history, and it has demonstrated that the Fund is already equipped with instruments that allow it to take quick and decisive action when no other means are available to prevent a crisis from turning into a catastrophe. But there have been a number of other large financial arrangements in recent months, most notably in support of programs of stabilization and reform in Argentina,

Russia, and Ukraine. Because of these and other actual and expected commitments, the Fund's liquidity position, adequate in 1995, is projected to weaken considerably over the next two years. The Fund's resources are probably sufficient for our normal business during this period, and if emergencies call for it the General Arrangements to Borrow (GAB) from some of our largest members can be activated.

But we must look beyond the next couple of years, since negotiations on quota size and shares are lengthy and require ratification by parliaments; we must take heed of the fact that the large and growing scale of international financial flows means that the financial resources needed to deal with crises will be larger than in the past; and we must see what action is needed to ensure that the Fund's resources are adequate to meet the demands that the Fund may face in the closing years of this century and beyond. This was agreed by our Interim Committee, and following their preliminary discussion and guidance we shall in the next few months be pursuing or considering a number of courses of action:

- the first and paramount priority is the next General Review of Fund Quotas, our members' capital subscriptions to the IMF. Fund quotas are the essential basis of our financial assistance to member countries. In relation to any of the usual measures of the size of the world economy, the size of the Fund as measured by quotas has declined continuously and substantially over the fifty years of its existence. The challenges presented by the globalized world economy point to an urgent need to reverse this decline. The next quota review is due to be completed by March 1998 at the latest. It must be initiated expeditiously, and in my view we should aim to complete the review before the end of 1996. The review should, in my assessment, lead roughly to a doubling in quotas, just to ensure that the size of the Fund keeps pace with the growth in the world economy since the last review and reflects to a modest extent the increased scale of international financial flows;

- second, we should be reviewing the role, size, and procedure for activation of the General Arrangements to Borrow and exploring ways to increase the potential resources available to the Fund through borrowing from our members in emergency situations. While considering these forms of borrowing, we must nevertheless ask ourselves how usable these resources would be in times of crisis, and how long it would take to activate them. In today's globalized markets, we must try to ensure that our capacity for reaction approaches the instant decision-making of investors if we want to have the ability truly to give confidence to markets and to our members;
- third, I believe that the special drawing rate (SDR) has an important role to play in the working of the system. A decision on an SDR allocation is overdue as far as equity for our thirty-seven new member countries is concerned, who have never received an allocation. We had difficult discussions in the fall of 1994 on this matter. A large majority of our members would prefer to proceed with an allocation on the basis of our present Articles of Agreement, recognizing that there is at present a long-term global need to supplement existing reserve assets; but an important minority have doubts about this and recommend an allocation under an amendment of our Articles, a lengthy and uncertain avenue. I fervently hope that a solution can be found, possibly by the combination of a general allocation and a collective decision by the industrial countries, for instance, that they would not use the SDRs that would be allocated to them. This would limit to a very strict minimum the liquidity effectively created.

Beyond this urgent equity issue, I hope we will be encouraged also to undertake a wide-ranging review of the role and function of the SDR, including the possibility of utilizing it for the financing of international financial safety-net arrangement, whereby SDRs could be issued on a temporary basis or lent to countries in support of strong policy programs in the context of liquidity crises.

More ambitiously, the perspective of globalization surely makes the question of the need for a central reserve asset issued by an international monetary authority much more relevant now and for the future. This would require a major reconsideration of the present characteristics of this instrument, as well as of the conditions required for its issuance. Discussion would then have to address questions that have up to now been left on the backburner, such as how the SDR could become the numeraire and provide the central anchor of the international monetary system. Distant as such a goal may be, it is not too early to have preliminary thoughts on such issues, and in particular on whether the SDR can be developed as an instrument to help achieve price stability, and to redefine its characteristics accordingly. This is certainly not a higher ambition than those that our founders dared to have fifty years ago;

- finally, we shall be exploring the possibility of developing arrangements for more orderly international debt adjustment, taking into account the experience with debt reorganization under national laws. In principle, such arrangements could reduce the need for official financial support. But consideration of this approach raises a number of complex economic, political, and legal issues, and I should emphasize that our work on this is still exploratory.

There are many other concerns I should have mentioned about how precisely I would like to see the IMF adapt itself to the challenges of this globalized world. Let me mention only the obvious: the need we see, together with our friends at the World Bank and the WTO, to face this world together in the closest possible cooperation. The IMF also wants to develop similar cooperation with the UN and, particularly, with the International Labour Organization (ILO) to face the many "post-chaos" situations in the world and to follow the orientations offered by the Copenhagen social summit.

June 1995

The Road Ahead
International Trade Policy in the Era of the World Trade Organization

RENATO RUGGIERO

There cannot be many individuals in Canada, or elsewhere for that matter, who combine Sylvia Ostry's extraordinary depth and breadth of experience in the area of trade, and economic policy more generally. Nor can there be many who match her record of excellence in her chosen field. Sylvia Ostry has served as a high official in her government, she has held a senior position in a prominent international institution – the Organization for Economic and Cultural Development (OECD) – and, from her academic vantage point, has made a signal contribution to our understanding of the complex world we live in. Many of the ideas and issues in the following essay have been influenced by Sylvia's work.

THE GLOBAL IMPERATIVE

It must be true that practically every generation in history has lived through change – be it social, economic, or political. And no doubt change has been viewed in every generation with a blend of apprehension and anticipation – apprehension at the discomfort it might represent, and anticipation at the opportunities it can offer. Some periods are more turbulent than others, but I wonder how many generations in years gone by have had to contend with the extraordinarily rapid change that characterizes our times.

What kind of change am I talking about, and what is driving it? The change I refer to is the dramatic internationalization, or globalization, of economic activity over the last two or three decades, and the profound political and social consequences that flow from this. A powerful confluence of forces drives globalization. Some of them no doubt reflect government policies but, more fundamentally, these are forces with a life of their own – forces unleashed by technological change, especially in the fields of transport and communications.

In economic terms, globalization means that production and trade have become inexorably intertwined. Production processes are spread across the globe. Producers must invest to trade and trade to invest. Most products entering the market today are either traded or heavily reliant on traded components for their production. The fact that trade plays a greater role in economic activity than it ever has before is easily discernible from statistics – trade flows have multiplied fifteen-fold in the last four decades, while production has increased six-fold. At the same time, dramatic increases have been registered in flows of foreign direct investment – in the ten years to 1993, investment flows worldwide quadrupled, to almost 200 billion dollars per annum. More and more jobs rely on trade, on the side of both imports and exports. All this has taken place against steadily rising living standards in many, but not all, countries. The fact that the benefits of globalization are yet to be globally enjoyed presents a policy challenge to which I shall return. However, no one should underestimate the extent to which global economic integration has helped, and is helping, to reduce poverty and marginalization. In the next few years two billion people in developing and transition economies are expected to enter the global marketplace, reinforcing the trends which have put a dozen or more developing countries among the world's most dynamic economies.

In political terms, globalization means that governments must learn to cooperate in more areas than in the past. Some of the distinctions we used to make between international policy and domestic policy look increasingly facile and irrelevant. Tensions naturally arise as governments are perceived as having an ever-more intrusive interest in each other's policies, and these tensions must be managed with deftness and political agility. As the domain of international rule-making and policy coordination expands, and the notion of "domestic" policy assumes a narrower focus, adequate care must be taken to safeguard diversity and preserve democracy. At the same time, defensive arguments based on sovereignty must be recognized for the illusion that they are. The true expression of sovereignty in today's world is in the capacity of democratically elected governments to articulate the interests of their constituents through negotiations and international commitments.

In social terms, managing globalization is also a major challenge. It is disingenuous to pretend that market-opening, continuing international economic integration, and trade liberalization will always be painless. Some people may well be displaced through the resource allocation shifts that occur as a result of these processes. But we should be clear about the whole picture. The efficiency gains from specialization through trade stimulate economic activity and create jobs, more than making up for what may be lost through job displacement. Managing this transition and dealing with the distributional consequences of change is a fundamental responsibility of governments, but definitely not one that will be met by shying away from the world marketplace.

Globalization will not go away. Policy-makers could not stop the process even if they wanted to. It is not something that is optional but a part of our normal everyday life in countless ways. The only real question is whether or not we accompany its advance with domestic policies which will help us adapt to the reality of change without an unbearable social cost.

Internationally, the choice is whether this inevitable process will take place within a system based on agreed rules or simply on power. In the post-war period we have generally tried to follow the first alternative. To abandon it now would change the economic – and possibly political – history for the world in a dangerous way for all its people.

THE WTO'S FIRST EIGHTEEN MONTHS: HIGHLIGHTS AND SHADOWS

Before turning to what I see as some of the major issues we need to address in the coming months and years, I would like to look briefly with you at the World Trade Organization's (WTO) first year and a half. It is a picture of light and shadow, of commitments implemented and others which remain still unfinished business.

The highlights include:

- *Implementation* of the Uruguay Round agreements: a good start has been made, but there is no room for complacency. The full and prompt implementation of commitments is essential for the credibility of the WTO and for building confidence on which to explore the trade agenda that lies ahead.
- *Dispute settlement*: we now have a more effective and credible mechanism for the resolution of trade disputes. So far, thirty-eight complaints have been brought to the WTO and a significant number of cases have been settled "out of court" – that is, resolved at the consultation stage which is an essential part of the procedure. This is strong testimony to the deterrent effect of the system.
- Establishment of the *Appellate Body*, whose first decision has just been handed down – a very difficult decision in view of the numerous criteria involved.

- *Increased membership:* the WTO now has 121 members. The fact that 29 countries are negotiating to join (including China and Russia) shows the vitality and the attraction of the multilateral system. Individual countries may join the WTO seeking economic benefits, but the global gain will also be more stable international relations. Clearly, we are close to realizing the long-sought goal of a multilateral trading system of universal membership, based not on weakened membership requirements but on a strengthened desire on the part of governments to participate fully in the globalizing world economy.
- *Trade and the environment:* the WTO's Committee on Trade and Environment has a wide-ranging agenda, which has been examined at some length by the committee. This discussion has provided a good basis for further progress in this important but often controversial area, both clarifying the issues at stake and bringing formerly divergent views closer together. In its report to the Ministerial Conference in Singapore, the committee will be in a position to better define areas for further examination and might be ready to suggest certain policy improvements to promote environmental concerns while at the same time enhancing or facilitating international trade.

The shadows appear when we recall that implementation also includes the commitment to continue negotiations in four important sectors of trade in services which was made at the end of the Uruguay Round. Now that we have at least an interim result on three of these – financial services, the movement of natural persons (those who provide services), and basic telecommunications – I would like to say something about what has been achieved – and what remains to be done.

You will remember that in July 1995 a negotiation on financial services ended with a muted or mitigated success: twenty-nine countries agreed to improve their commitments under the General Agreement on Trade in Services (GATS), but the US found the package unsatisfactory and was unable to make any offer as to future access to its financial services market. The negotiations will be resumed in 1997 and then I hope, and expect, an improved package, with the US as a full participant, will be agreed upon. In the negotiations on basic telecommunications, which ended on 30 April 1996, a very interesting and worthwhile harvest of market opening offers, plus substantial progress in the area of competition and the behaviour of state monopolies, was achieved. But again it was impossible to finalize the deal, because the US considered the result unsatisfactory. The negotiators agreed to preserve the results achieved so far with the objective that they be improved further in a brief period of renewed negotiations in January/February 1997, and the date of 1 January 1998 be maintained for their entry into force. I believe this process too will be brought to a successful conclusion in 1997.

The fourth sectoral negotiation, on maritime transport, is now in progress. It, too, is facing difficulty, following a statement by the US that it will not make an offer in the light of its assessment of the offers made by others. We must ensure that an acceptable result can nevertheless be reached by the end of June 1996, but it will not be easy.

It is too early to draw up a balance sheet. But I think one preliminary conclusion, at least, can be drawn. It is not impossible for negotiation in a single sector to produce worthwhile – even surprisingly good – results. The telecoms negotiations proved that – and in my opinion the results in financial services were also much better than might have been expected from a short negotiation in a single, highly sensitive sector.

Of course we should not underestimate the impact of missing the date of 30 April 1996 for the formal conclusion of the telecom negotiations, or of the result so far in financial services. But it would be equally wrong to overstate the case. The history of international negotiations – especially trade negotiations – is full of missed targets. If we allow every such instance to become a drama we only make it harder to go on to eventual success.

One final comment: these negotiations became classed as unfinished business because it was not possible to bring them to resolution even in the magic moment of the end of the Uruguay Round. So by definition they must be considered among the hardest cases. It is thus no wonder that they could not be settled in one further attempt – but up to now none has been an outright failure. This is all the more reason we cannot accept a failure in the maritime sector.

THE ROAD TO SINGAPORE

It is against this background of light and shadow that preparation is underway for the WTO's first ministerial meeting, which will be held in Singapore in December 1996. Certainly the ministerial will provide a chance to take stock of what has been achieved after two years, but the concentration of political force it represents could be wasted if we do not also have more ambitious goals. Let me outline some possible areas where I think it is realistic to expect Singapore to help the multilateral system to move forward as it must.

One such area is *further liberalization* in goods and services trade – and through improvements in the trade rules. There is a debate on what further liberalization can really mean. Some delegations do not want to change the commitments already made at the end of the Uruguay Round and prefer to keep the time-horizon of 1999 or 2000. Some others, on the contrary, suggest considering possibilities that include accelerated or additional tariff reductions, further work on professional services, and working towards the harmonization of technical standards and the simplification of rules of origin. Other possibilities will no doubt emerge as we continue the preparatory discussions.

The discussions that are going on among a number of countries over liberalizing trade in information technology are a particularly encouraging development, one which should also complement and reinforce the opening-up of telecommunications services. I hope that any eventual agreement will be made on a multilateral basis, to make the most of its benefits both to the global economy and the trading system.

As far as *investment* is concerned, globalization has dramatically reduced the utility of distinctions that policy makers used to maintain between different forms of market access. In this setting, it seems to me that no rationale can be offered for not having multilateral investment rules while we have multilateral trade rules. In the Uruguay Round, the negotiation on trade-related investment measures – or TRIMS – resulted in a mandate to look at investment issues with a view to considering whether the TRIMS Agreement should be complemented with provisions on investment. At the same time, negotiations in the field of trade in services have led to substantive commitments on investment in a wide range of sectors. These commitments apply to the right of foreign investors to establish themselves, as well as to conduct business once they are established. In addition to these sector-specific undertakings, WTO members are committed to providing most favoured nation (MFN) treatment with respect to all trade in all services, except in the relatively few cases where narrow exceptions to MFN have been inscribed.

Notwithstanding the significance of what we have already achieved in services, I believe we need a more horizontal and all-encompassing approach to investment in the WTO, particularly as nothing has been done so far in the sphere of goods. Multilateral rules in this area should build on the WTO principles of MFN and national treatment, thereby contributing to a policy environment that encourages and safeguards foreign investment, especially in the great majority of developing and least-developed countries who are at present largely outside the main flows of foreign direct investment. The OECD, as well as some regional trade agreements, have already developed, or are in the process of developing, international investment rules. But I believe governments will increasingly recognize the need for work on this issue in a more global setting.

There is a risk, in the absence of a strong multilateral framework, of an accumulation of potentially inconsistent and even discriminatory regimes with regard to foreign investment. The question is how to ensure a truly multilateral dimension to this question that takes account not only of the role of investment within the international trading system but also of the common interest that both industrial and developing countries have in ensuring a favourable investment climate. It is hard to imagine that an answer can be found outside the WTO. There are currently more than 900 bilateral investment treaties. If all countries in the world were to participate in such agreements, we would need around 20,000 bilateral treaties. This fact provides a clear answer to those who preach the superiority of a bilateral approach. I cannot image that business would welcome such a bewildering variety of requirements. It is clearly preferable to have just one set, covering all countries, developed and developing alike, under the same rules and disciplines and with just one enforcement procedure.

The TRIMS Agreement also contains a mandate to consider the need for rules on *competition policy*. The General Agreement on Tariffs and Trade (GATT) and the WTO have sought to enhance competition for the last fifty years through promoting trade liberalization. More explicitly, competition questions were taken up in the Havana Charter and came onto the Uruguay Round agenda through the negotiations on basic telecommunications. I believe it is important for us to examine this question thoroughly in the WTO setting. As government mandated and supported policies have become less trade-restricting, attention focuses increasingly on market barriers maintained by enterprises – that is, barriers that are intrinsic to the structure of markets and independent of any government policy.

We need to determine, firstly, how pervasive and problematic such barriers may be. Secondly, we must ask whether they should be dealt with nationally or whether we need international disciplines to ensure the proper functioning of markets. And if we do need an international approach, what should it be? Should we create a right of multilateral action that commits government to implementing their national competition policies, or should we go further and write substantive competition rules? These are interesting and important questions that we must address. We can certainly learn something from the negotiations on basic telecommunications, where governments clearly felt the need to spell out and commit themselves to specific, multilateral pro-competitive principles.

Whether or not we recognize it, competition is making itself part of our agenda. It is just a question of when and how this becomes explicit.

Beyond the built-in agenda, issues that have been proposed by some countries include *trade and labour standards* (the most potentially controversial of all these subjects). No one can deny the importance of the core labour standards that have been internationally agreed. But the issue is now about the extent of the relationship with trade and the best forum for discussion. That is why this issue remains potentially divisive. There is a shared responsibility to avoid a dramatization of it at the Ministerial Conference. If this were to happen, it is certain that the people whose interests we all want to protect would not be in any better position.

Proposals also include the problem of *corruption* in international trade, which has been linked with the need for further work on *government procurement*, the question of *regionalism*, and the adaptation of the trade rules to the global economy. The issue of the effects of commodity prices, exchange rates, and debt on *developing-country trade earnings* has been raised verbally.

These suggestions need to be approached with objectivity and care, in line with the principle of consensus which has always guided the multilateral system. Developing a consensus in these areas will be a serious challenge – but the multilateral trading system has successfully met such challenges in the past (for example, when services and environment were brought into the picture).

One of the most notable changes on the world trading scene in the last decade or so has been the death of the North-South divide – an event as significant as the demolition of the Berlin Wall. This change is attributable in large measure to the embrace of market-opening and liberalization policies in countries at all levels of development. A priority for Singapore is to sustain this new unity.

If we are to move forward to develop a trade agenda for the twenty-first century, it is essential to have a solid base of confidence among all the members of the trading system that it is working in their interests.

THE CHALLENGES AHEAD

Shaping the trading system of the new century means, above all, responding to four fundamental challenges.

The first is to do a better job than we are doing at present in conveying to people everywhere the message that open trade and the multilateral system work in their interest. We have to recognize that the rapid advance of global integration has contributed to a climate of uncertainty in many societies, a situation which is ripe for exploitation by those who peddle the quack remedies of protectionism and xenophobia. What is urgently needed is for governments, the private sector, and academics to work together to restate clearly and persuasively the truth that the past fifty years of our history makes so evident – that open trade within the rules of the multilateral system is the key to growth, and hence to all our hopes of a more prosperous and stable existence.

The second challenge is to respect and strengthen the fundamental contract that now unites countries at all levels of economic development. The industrialized world has to keep open its markets and improve their openness in the years ahead. On their side, the developing countries have to continue with their liberalizing reforms and increase their integration into the global system. And together, both industrialized and developing countries have to work to improve the situation of the least-developed.

I believe that raising living standards in these countries is one of the most urgent tasks before us. It has been estimated that while incomes per head are expected to rise by 80 per cent on average in East Asia between 1996 and the year 2005, the comparable figure for Sub-Saharan Africa is only 8 per cent. How can we help to narrow this widening gap and to promote development in the poorest countries?

At the very least, we must ensure that all markets are completely and securely open to the goods and services produced by these countries. A commitment to bind all tariffs that they face at zero and eliminate all remaining quantitative restrictions on their exports by a firm date would be one useful initiative. There are many other ways in which we could assist, such as improving their access to investment (another reason for taking this issue up in the WTO), encouraging regional initiatives among least-developed countries, and applying more flexible rules of origin to their products.

Equally important is building up their institutional and human capacity so that they are fully able to take advantage of improved opportunities. This calls for some fresh approaches, both in the cooperation among agencies providing technical assistance and in the means by which they do so.

The WTO has made a start in this direction, by developing an integrated technical cooperation plan with the United Nations Conference on Trade and Development (UNCTAD) and the International Trade Centre, which we jointly sponsor. There is clearly more to be done in promoting such cooperation. We must also work closely together with all other relevant agencies to exploit to the full the opportunities new communications technology offers to extend the scope and the lasting impact of our capacity-building efforts.

Lastly, there is a need to pay serious attention to the situation of net food-importing developing countries who – for a variety of reasons – are facing rising prices for a number of agricultural commodities.

The third challenge is universality – the need to bring China, Russia, and all the other countries still outside into the WTO system. We can only reap the full benefit of a rule-based global trading system when this is achieved. No one is under any illusion that the process is an easy one. The accession of large transition economies, in particular, raises significant questions of substance whose answers need to strike an acceptable balance among the aspirations of the candidate countries, the interests of existing members, and the need to safeguard the integrity of the system and its rules. There is no quick political fix to these issues. Aspiring and existing members alike share the responsibility of ensuring that the accession negotiations proceed as rapidly as possible but in a way which strengthens the system as a whole.

The fourth challenge is to make sense of the relationship between regionalism and the multilateral trading system. It is less than fifteen years since the dramatic explosion in regional agreements occurred, making such arrangements the prominent feature of international economic relations that they are today. In 1980, relatively few customs unions and free trade areas existed, but now nearly all WTO members belong to one or more regional trading arrangements. Apart from the European Community, what arrangements there were fifteen yeas ago tended to be limited in scope and to focus primarily, if not exclusively, on preferential tariffs. The new wave of regional trading arrangements can be said, like so many things, to have started in North America.

Indeed, Canada played a pivotal and initiating role in the establishment of a free trade agreement in North America, which was soon to be extended as the North American Free Trade Agreement (NAFTA). And now there are plans for a hemispheric free trade agreement, which would also build on existing arrangements in South America, such as MERCOSUR, the ANDEAN Pact, and the Central American Common Market. In Asia, we see ASEAN expanding its geographical coverage and deepening the integration process. The South Asian countries are also developing a regional arrangement. And, of course, we have APEC, which, while not as yet involving trade preferences among its members, embodies an ambitious vision of free trade among countries in Asia and also across the Pacific Basin to North and South America. In Africa, several regional arrangements are being developed. In Europe, the European Union has built up a complex hierarchy of preferential arrangements involving all its immediate neighbours and has wider schemes in prospect. The idea of a Trans-Atlantic free trade agreement has also recently attracted considerable attention.

The regional liberalizing impulse is not in itself cause for alarm among the upholders of the multilateral system. Regional initiatives can contribute significantly to the development of multilateral rules and commitments, and in regions such as Sub-Saharan Africa they may be an essential starting-point for integration of least-developed countries into the wider global economy. At the most basic level, the real split is between liberalization, at whatever level, and protectionism. Viewed from this perspective, regional and multilateral initiatives should be on the same side, mutually supportive and reinforcing.

However, the sheer size and ambition of recent regional initiatives means we can no longer take this complementarity for granted, if indeed we ever could. We need a clear statement of principles, backed by firm commitments, to ensure that regional schemes do not act as a centrifugal force, pulling the multilateral system apart.

The answer is to be found, I suggest, in the principle which some of the newer regional groupings have enunciated – *Open Regionalism*. Of course, we need to be clear about what open regionalism means. Among the different possibilities, I see two basic alternatives.

The first is to ensure that any preferential area under consideration will be *consistent* with the legal requirements of the multilateral system. The existing provisions mean that such areas could at the same time be legally compatible with the WTO's rules and preferential in their nature, which means they can be an exception to the MFN clause that is the basic principle of the multilateral system. The possibility of making such a legal exception to the MFN principle within the rules was conceived in a completely different time and situation. Today, with the proliferation of regional groupings, the exception could become the rule, and this would risk changing completely the nature of the system.

The second interpretation of open regionalism is the one I hear from a number of governments including some members of APEC or MERCOSUR. In this scenario, the gradual elimination of internal barriers to trade within a regional grouping will be implemented at more or less the same rate and on the same timetable as the lowering of barriers towards non-members. This would mean that regional liberalization would in practice as well as in law be generally consistent with the MFN principle.

The choice between these alternatives is a critical one: they point to very different outcomes. In the first case, the point at which we would arrive in no more than twenty to twenty-five years would be a division of the trading world into two or three intercontinental preferential areas, each with its own rules and with free trade inside the area, but with external barriers still existing among the blocs.

Is this the sort of world any of us would want?

I leave you to imagine the consequences of this vision in terms of world stability and security: where, for example, would China and Russia be in such a world?

The second alternative, on the other hand, points towards the gradual *convergence* of regionalisms and multilateralism on the basis of shared aims and principles; first and foremost, respect of the MFN principle. At the end, we would have one free global market with rules and disciplines internationally agreed and applied to all, with the capacity to invoke the respect of the rights and obligations to which all had freely subscribed. In such a world there could and must be a place for China, Russia, and all the other candidates to the WTO.

Given the reality of regionalism, and the necessity to maintain the central importance of the multilateral system, the question comes down to how best to ensure this gradual convergence takes place. Should it, for example, be left to concerted unilateral effort or be the subject of a multilateral negotiation, in the same way as past enlargements of the European Community helped spark previous GATT Rounds? Should we attempt to set a time-limit within which regional liberalization of market access would be followed either by its extension on an MFN basis or the start of multilateral negotiations? Where regional groupings establish new trade rules, should we seek to agree on a mechanism and a time frame under which they would be brought into full conformity with the multilateral rules where they exist? In cases where there are as yet no equivalent WTO rules we will need to consider a timetable for negotiating their multilateral application.

Maintaining the primacy of the WTO's rules and dispute-settlement system is vital, not as an end in itself but in order to avoid a bedlam of competing and contradictory jurisdictions. As I mentioned earlier, the current evolution of rules on investment gives some early warning of what this could be like. If we do not uphold the primacy of the multilateral rules, we risk seeing a form of Gresham's Law operating in dispute settlement, with weaker rules driving out stronger as governments choose the jurisdiction which most favours their case.

Obviously the mechanisms by which we assure the convergence of regional and multilateral systems needs a great deal of further thought. I am hopeful that the WTO Committee on Regional Trading Agreements, under the very able chairmanship of Canada's ambassador to the WTO, John Weekes, will make an important contribution to this process. For now, the important point is to be clear about the necessity of this convergence.

It comes down to a question of the sort of world we want to live in. Do we want a world where the advance of global economic integration is matched by a global framework of agreed trade rules which ensure openness and foster growth with stability? Or do we want a power-based system where competing blocs attempt to regionalize the global economy with all the economic and political stresses that would entail?

I make no apology for putting the choice so starkly in terms of alternative visions. If the multilateral system is not animated by a positive and challenging vision of its future how can it hope to maintain dynamism and direction? Regional schemes have more often than not a political vision guiding the trade initiatives and, in many cases, a clear timetable as well. Why should the multilateral system be any less ambitious?

CONCLUSION

The challenges I have outlined are contributing to a growing awareness that trade is not just a technical question, but a matter of high political importance. In the WTO, the world now has a permanent trade policy forum as well as a more effective means of negotiating commitments and making and enforcing trade rules. Trade and trade policy have been put back in the front row of international concerns, where they were intended to be by the architects of the post-war international institutions. With the establishment of the WTO, and the conclusion – expected very soon – of comprehensive agreements for cooperation at every level with the World Bank and the International Monetary Fund (IMF), the matrix of trade and finance and development is not only completed but updated to contribute to global prosperity and stability in the new century. This improved institutional cooperation is a major step towards fulfilling the mandate given to the WTO by governments to work for improved coherence in international economic policy-making.

The WTO has been invited for the first time to participate, with the Bank, the Fund, and the United Nations, in the G7 Summit of leaders of the major industrialized economies, which will be held in 1996 in Lyon at the end of April. This recognition of the importance of the multilateral system is very welcome not only for itself but also because of the opportunity it gives to reinforce the trade dimension in growth and development for countries at all economic levels. Many of the themes that will be before the G7 leaders will follow from the summit that Canada hosted in Halifax in 1995. The fact of globalization will be the backdrop to the summit's deliberations, as it is to every serious economic discussion. It is my hope that the WTO, whose business is with the lifeblood of global integration – trade – can help bring concrete and practical answers to the questions that surround this process, especially the extension of its benefits to those who are currently on the economic margins.

At the end of 1997, the multilateral trading system will be fifty years old. I would like to see this anniversary properly observed; not just as a recognition of what the system has meant for growth and stability in the world since 1947 but as a reaffirmation of its value for the present and the future. Precisely how and where such a commemoration should take place is a question for further discussion, possibly by ministers at the Singapore meeting in December. But I believe we should not waste such an opportunity to renew at a high political level our commitment to the system which is the foundation of our present prosperity and our future prospects.

Someone observed to me recently that Canadians have multilateralism in their DNA, and it is certainly true that Canada's contribution to the multilateral principle, whether in economic or political affairs, has been an outstanding one. The most recent expression of this was, of course, Canada's lead in advocating the establishment of the WTO at the end of the Uruguay Round. I know that NAFTA and other regional initiatives have assumed an increased importance in the Canadian policy landscape and in

Canadian economic life, but I am confident that Canada will take the lead in demonstrating that there is no contradiction between the active development of regional opportunities and a continuing firm commitment to the multilateral principle. In this, as in so many other ways, Sylvia Ostry's influence will continue to be felt.

May 1996

Prospects for Greater Hemispheric Economic Cooperation
An Opportunity for Canada

ENRIQUE V. IGLESIAS

INTRODUCTION

In the world of international trade and economic relations, Sylvia Ostry has made many significant contributions. Therefore, I consider it a great honour to have been asked to share with you some perspectives on the relationship between Latin American and the Caribbean and Canada – past, present, and future.

Latin America and the Caribbean have long been thought of in the broader world as an area where countries have particularly strong economic and political ties to the US. While the perception of the US's overwhelming presence is no doubt largely true, Canada has long had a special relationship with the Caribbean. In fact, Canadian trade with the region dates from the 1660s when New France, under the leadership of Jean Talon, exported fish products, lumber, and beer to French territories in the West Indies. Today, the most visible manifestation of this enduring special relationship is the "CARIBCAN program," Canada's non-reciprocal trade regime for the Caribbean, which was adopted in 1986.

With the end of the Cold War, a new era began in Latin America and the Caribbean. Political and economic relations are being redefined throughout the region and new opportunities arise for many countries to play an active role in the region. Canada is one of the countries actively seizing initiatives and seeking to build constructive relationships throughout the Americas and this became especially intensive in the 1990s. Canada has provided substantial aid and technical assistance through national and inter-American institutions, supported otherwise underfunded projects, developed educational exchange initiatives, and, most prominently, has been central to moving forth the process of establishing a Western Hemisphere free trade area through the Free Trade Area of the Americas (FTAA) initiative. Over the next decade or so, we will see if Canada's intensified engagement with the rest of the hemisphere underscores a broader intellectual shift away from the traditional idea of the country as an extension of Europe toward the idea of Canada as a country of the Americas, with a uniquely "New World" outlook and set of experiences to offer.

THE IMPORTANCE OF RECENT CHANGES IN CANADA–LATIN AMERICA RELATIONS

If one key event can be said to have marked the beginning of Canada's active engagement in the hemisphere it was the decision to join the Organization of American States (OAS) in the late 1980s. While Canada has long been an important member of the Inter-American Development Bank, traditionally it avoided participation in the OAS, strictly a hemispheric forum. However, as the Cold War was ending and democracies returned to Latin America, Canada came to see the possibility of playing a valuable and influential role in a transforming hemisphere. From the beginning, it took an active role in all facets of OAS operations and brought to the table a fresh, different, and unique outlook.

The beginning of Canada's expanded economic engagement with the rest of the hemisphere can be dated to early 1991 with the announcement of negotiations for a North American Free Trade Agreement (NAFTA), which involved Mexico. While a free trade agreement between Canada and the United States had been in place since 1989, Canada had had little trade with Mexico. With the launch of the NAFTA negotiations, many Canadian firms began looking at opportunities in Latin America for the first time. The focus initially was on Mexico. Canada's total trade (imports and exports) with Mexico grew from US$1.5 billion in 1988 to US$3.3 billion in 1994 to US$5.9 billion in 1998. The momentum created by the entry into force of the NAFTA at the beginning of 1994 led to Canada playing a leading role in the launch of the FTAA process at the Miami Summit of the Americas at the end of 1994. In 1996, Canada further advanced links with the region by signing a bilateral free trade agreement with Chile. More recently, at the end of January of 2000, Canada and Costa Rica announced that they would explore the possibility of negotiating a free trade agreement. The result of these free trade initiatives is that Canada's trade with Latin America and the Caribbean has grown substantially over the past ten years. In 1988, the value of Canada's total trade with its partners in the Americas (excluding the United States) was approximately US$5.5 billion. By 1994, this figure had grown to US$8.6 billion and by 1998 the total topped US$12 billion. These figures also reflect the fact that Latin American and Caribbean countries have increased their exports to the Canadian market; indeed, the region overall enjoys a trade surplus with Canada.

WHAT HAS CANADA BROUGHT TO THE REGION RECENTLY?

A general impression about Canada in the hemisphere is that it is a country unlike any other in the Americas. It is an economically developed middle power that functions internally on the basis of a social paradigm that gives strong consideration to equity and which works. In addition, externally it has no tradition as a military power.

Canada can draw on this paradigm as it becomes more constructively engaged in the region on many levels. In doing so, the most important asset that Canada has brought to the table is arguably its experience of being a "small" country vis à vis the United States, yet one that has long successfully pursued an independent course in the world. Canada's experience in successfully negotiating with the US is a focus of interest for Latin American and many other countries. What is most impressive and valuable from a Latin American and Caribbean perspective is to observe how Canada consistently rises to the occasion. As the process of hemispheric integration has developed, the nations of Latin America and the Caribbean have increasingly made common cause with Canada in their efforts to find new equilibrium and balance in hemispheric relations. This has proven to be a "win-win" process for all countries involved.

The experience that Canada has consistently used in pursuing its international objectives is multilateralism, while simultaneously recognizing that its priority is its bilateral relationship with the US. By working together with other like-minded countries, Canada is able to both further the global public good and to work for the establishment of universally applicable rules. This experience of trying to integrate regional and multilateral objectives is also valuable for countries in the region and it is once again at the centre of debate today. The FTAA, which seeks to liberalize commerce from Nunavut to Tierra del Fuego, is arguably the most important economic initiative in the history of the Americas. In 1999 Canada finished an eighteen-month stint as chair of the overall process. During its term, Canada oversaw the launch of active negotiations on all issues, the setting up of the FTAA Secretariat, and the fulfillment of the mandate to achieve concrete progress by the year 2000 through the adoption of certain business facilitation measures. The Canadian presidency culminated with the successful hosting of the Fifth Americas Business Forum and the Fifth FTAA Ministerial meeting in Toronto in November 1999. The Bank joined Canada in this endeavour through its support of the FTAA in the context of the Organization of American States (OAS), the Inter-America Development Bank (IDB), the Economic Commission for Latin America and the Caribbean (ECLAC) Tripartite Committee. All Latin America and the Caribbean were extremely grateful for Canada's effective chair in the critical launch of the FTAA negotiations and especially to Katherine McCallion who worked so hard and effectively leading the FTAA's executive arm, the Trade Negotiations Committee.

As Canada's trade performance vis à vis Latin America and the Caribbean has greatly improved over the last ten years, Canadian firms are taking a new look at this once neglected market. Over the next ten years, the potential of the region as a consumer of Canadian exports and as a producer of products in globally integrated supply chains is enormous. Consider some facts, on which I will expand later, about where Latin America and the Caribbean are in 2000:

- it is a market of 500 million people;
- disincentives to trade, which existed in the region fifteen years ago, have been dismantled;
- twenty free trade agreements have been signed and four customs unions have been formed or re-activated in the past ten years and a considerable number of new agreements are in different stages of negotiation;
- the foreign investment codes in the region are among the most liberal in the world.

With much progress made in reforming the economies in Latin America and the Caribbean, the region is well-positioned to resume strong growth in the years ahead. But we also have important challenges and Canada's experience in some of these issues can prove very useful for our countries.

LESSONS FOR LATIN AMERICA FROM THE CANADIAN ECONOMIC AND SOCIAL EXPERIENCE

When economists look at Canada in recent years, one of its most impressive achievements has been the fiscal discipline it has demonstrated in transforming its large budget deficits into the large surpluses it is enjoying today. The approach to recent fiscal discipline can be of particular interest to Latin American countries as it has been implemented in the context of other important structural reforms. Lessons can be learned on consistency of objectives vis à vis reforming taxation (including simple and efficient revenue collection systems), defining priority fiscal expenditure, eliminating distorting factors on relative prices, and opening up the economy. Canada has undertaken major reforms in the past ten years, not without pain, in all of these areas. Labour market reforms and human resources training have also been important. In effect, Canada must adjust, but preserve, its long tradition of social protection and equity in the face of the pressures of globalization. Latin America and the Caribbean also urgently need programs that increase the efficient operation of labour markets and the modernization of training programs for all sectors of our society while providing social protection for the most vulnerable groups. The region also can review Canada's experience for lessons on institutional stability, modernization of public institutions, and overall integration of policy-making.

Another area where the "Canadian way" can serve as a global model is in the field of financial regulation. The country's banking system is among the most stable in the world. Since 1923, Canada has experienced only two bank failures. Nevertheless, stability has not bred complacency. Canadian banks have aggressively applied new technologies and have looked outside their own borders for new opportunities. Scotiabank, for example, is becoming a household name in some Latin American countries as branches have sprung up from the Dominican Republic to Argentina. The Canadian experience shows that one can have both a highly stable domestic banking system and a globally competitive international banking sector.

With respect to handling the interaction between the trade initiatives on the regional and global level, Canada has struggled to come up with consistency of objectives and this is an important lesson for Latin America. Concurrent with the General Agreement on Tariffs and Trade (GATT) Uruguay Round negotiations, Canada successfully negotiated the North American Free Trade Agreement. While such a complex undertaking posed tremendous challenges, a key issue is how to transform a potential liability into strength. In Canada's case, it seems that harmonization of objectives is developed in a practical way with a strategy to establish first its bottom line on each issue and then to seek to maximize its gains in the forum that offers the most potential for success. This sounds simple on the surface. However, it takes a significant amount of experience to be able to do this well as the issue should not only be maximization of individual country goals but essentially to contribute to a universal trading system based on rules.

Social and economic equality is another major challenge for Latin America today. This is one of the most pressing challenges facing our region; indeed Canada's David Pollock, a great Canadian who has devoted his entire life to the economic and social development of Latin America and the Caribbean, rightly termed this as the region's "supreme challenge." Canada is a shining light in a hemisphere where, with a few exceptions, the gap between rich and poor is wide. Poverty and inequality lie at the heart of most of the region's social problems. While Canada is a wealthier country than those in Latin America and the Caribbean, and hence has more resources to distribute, the key to success in the social field is its underlying belief that poverty is a national and a community problem as well as an individual problem. We think Canada's way of organizing an overall system of social development has many lessons. These encompass tax policy, fiscal policy, funding of core programs in health, education, and human resources development, regional development programs, labour market policies, and income support programs.

In another area, one of the most important developments in the Canadian economy in recent years has been the emergence of the high-technology sector. This experience is important for Latin America and the Caribbean which, like Canada, does not want to be overly dependent on natural resource exploitation. The difficulties associated with this type of economic structure are well known. What is really important about the success of Canada in transforming itself into an information-age economy is that it offers a model to others seeking to move up the value-added chain.

In addition to the high-tech economy per se, Canada has also been a leader in the application of technology to formerly "low-tech" activities. From fishing to farming to forestry, computers, satellites, remote communication equipment, and the like, new technologies are widely applied. The "information revolution" in these and other sectors has increased productivity and improved environmental management. Canada has much to offer in moving to apply these types of approaches to similar industries in Latin America and the Caribbean.

The last area I wish to touch on where Canada can be seen to offer valuable lessons is on specific areas of economic policy management, particularly monetary and exchange-rate policy. The Canadian experience in monetary and exchange policy is interesting and useful for our countries. In some Latin American countries, recent experience has included many stabilization programs, but ones in which there has been heavy reliance on high interest rates with not much flexibility for currency fluctuation. This has sometimes tended to exacerbate other problems, including slow growth and "exit." A prolonged use of the exchange rate as a nominal anchor for inflation also frequently resulted in overvalued currencies and higher trade and current account deficits. With a different experience, as a small open economy highly dependent on trade, Canada has been able to implement a more flexible exchange-rate system, but one in which monetary goals are the essential policy targets.

Monetary policy in Canada is defined by a long-term goal of achieving and maintaining price stability. Intermediate nominal targets are at present used to guide monetary policy over the short and medium terms and inflation-reduction targets (1 to 3 per cent range) have been set in recent years. As noted before, in the case of Canada and other countries with flexibility in their exchange-rate regimes, monetary policy is directed at affecting other variables, such as monetary and credit aggregates. The implementation of Canada's policy has resulted in inflation declining to desired levels and the easing of monetary conditions, with important declines in both interest rates and depreciation of the exchange rate. Also, with wage and price inflation under control, nominal depreciation has resulted in real depreciation. And given the combined effect of being a small open economy which has strong links to a large and growing economy, this policy has been a key in contributing to the reactivation of growth in recent years and the development of an increasingly dynamic export sector in the hard-fought North American market. This inflation targeting policy has the common automatic stabilization mechanism of tightening monetary conditions in the case of an increase in the rate of inflation (price demand pressure) and vice versa. The system also allows major price movements resulting from supply shocks to affect the price level but not the rate of inflation. In this way, the system allows for monetary policy response to supply shocks.

In Latin America, lower inflation recently has also allowed a number of countries to move to more flexible exchange-rate regimes. A key concern in introducing policy change has been reduction of current-account deficits and flexibility to manœuvre in the face of volatile capital flows and commodity prices. Some countries (Mexico and Brazil) have moved from semi-fixed to floating exchange rates. Other countries have either devalued or widened bands in which their currencies are allowed to float. Other countries have moved beyond the question of fixed exchange-rate regimes and have considered currency boards or even abandoning local currencies. On the latter, the two main alternatives that have been discussed are the adoption of regional or sub-regional currencies, or, alternatively, dollarization. I believe a regional currency makes sense for deep integration schemes such as the Southern Common Market (MERCOSUR) Agreement. Discussion of these issues is just beginning and more time is needed to continue evaluating the appropriate exchange rate options for a country or subregions.

Finally, I would also like to mention in passing that Canada also has an important experience to share with Latin America in the area of exploiting and preserving the vitality of a multicultural society. This is important for our region as we also have enriching cultural diversity but still need to find ways to nourish it and to promote equality within it.

Allow me now to move to another important matter of our hemispheric relations. I would like to focus now on the question of what Latin American and Caribbean countries have to offer to Canada. In my view, the region offers Canada significant opportunities for trade, investment, and cooperation in international policy issues. In fact, many of these opportunities exist as a result of common features that can be found in the economies of Canada and those in various parts of Latin America and the Caribbean. For example, Canada and many countries in the region are small open economies that depend on exports to foreign markets to sustain economic growth. Other common features include the important role that exploiting natural resources plays in economic development; the presence of high levels of foreign direct investment (FDI) from multinational firms, and a high degree of integration or interaction with the US economy. Let me link some of these issues to the question of what trade opportunities Latin America offers to Canada.

If we consider domestic markets according to population size, Latin America has important markets to offer to Canada on a regional or country basis. These markets are comparable to other international markets, of course, taking into account the level of per capita income and consumption. With respect to markets in Latin America and the Caribbean, however, a key issue that needs to be kept in mind is the expanding size of its large market, the abundance of human and natural resources, and a vast range of investment opportunities. Import demand in Latin America and the Caribbean is potentially very high, particularly if there is some improvement in the current distribution of income.

At present, with a population close to 500 million inhabitants, the Latin American and Caribbean region is a market of very significant dimensions. Regional markets are represented by MERCOSUR with 210 million, the Andean region with 109 million, Central America with 31 million, and the Caribbean with 6 million. Mexico is a market of 96 million and Chile of 15 million. These figures show that Latin America and the Caribbean have a population more that 1.7 times the size of the United States and 1.3 times the size of the European Union. Moreover, there is a more dynamic demographic trend in Latin America and the Caribbean than any developed country and many affinities abound among the countries in terms of history, language, culture, and tastes.

Another way of understanding the economic importance of the region as a business destination is by reviewing the FDI flows that Latin America and the Caribbean have been able to attract in recent years. Due to the turbulence in international markets produced by the Asian and Brazilian financial crises, FDI flows to developing countries in the aggregate have declined over the past two years. However, Latin America and the Caribbean alone have defied this trend. Total FDI flows to the region in 1998 reached a record US$77 billion and the preliminary number for 1999 shows inflows of US$86 billion. In addition, on the all-important question of distribution of FDI flows among developing regions of the world, Latin America and the Caribbean have almost completely closed the gap with Asia by attracting 41 per cent of FDI total flows, compared with 44 per cent for Asia and 15 per cent for other developing countries. These new all-time records for FDI flows are particularly important given that they were reached during a period of significant international financial instability and at a time when Brazil, Latin America's large economy, was mired in a severe economic crisis. The durability of Latin America and the Caribbean through this period of crisis bodes very well for the region's long-term economic prospects.

As I mentioned previously, there is already an important level overall two-way trade between Canada and Latin America and the Caribbean. However, in order to underscore the specific benefits to Canada, I would like explore the evolution of Canadian exports to the regional market over the past ten years. Canada's total exports to Latin American and Caribbean markets rose from US$2.2 billion in 1988 to US$3.5 billion in 1998. Markets of particular importance were Mexico, where Canadian exports increased from US$403 million in 1988 to US$857 million in 1998, and MERCOSUR, where Canadian exports jumped from US$482 million to US$1.1 billion over the same period.

While the Canadian private sector deserves great credit for these export gains, I believe that we need to reflect on the question of whether Canada is currently realizing its full potential with the region. I happen to believe that there are conditions for a much more significant level of trade to take place. Let me explain why this is the case. As many of you know, over the past decade Canada has deepened the concentration of its exports bound to the US market. In fact, the US share in total Canadian exports has now gone beyond 85 per cent. This has meant that the share of total Canadian exports to all other regions in the world, including Latin America, has decreased. This is an important result and underscores the tremendous effect of the Canada-US Free Trade Agreement and NAFTA. Far from being a negative development though, it suggests an opportunity. As the Free Trade Area of the Americas is negotiated and enters into force, the totality of markets in Latin America and the Caribbean will be fully open to Canadian exports. Hence, Canada's exports to the region are likely to increase significantly. In fact, the diversification of trade resulting from the FTAA has the potential to generate the "third option" that Canadian trade policy-makers have long sought. While the direction of Canada's trade is likely to shift more toward Latin America and the Caribbean after the entry into force of the FTAA in 2005, the most important result in this initiative will be an overall increase in total intra-hemispheric trade, including Canada and the United States.

Between 1989 and 1998, the average rate of growth of Canadian exports with Latin America was 2.4 per cent per year. There are several reasons that help to explain the increase in exports that has already taken place. One clear reason is that the large Latin American market resumed growth in the 1990s and re-established its position over the past decade as one of the most dynamic areas in the world for trade and investment. The implementation of ambitious economic reform programs and improvements in macroeconomic stability also contributed to more investment and trade exchange.

Another important reason is the strong trade and investment links that exist between countries in the region and the US economy. From the latter, it should be expected that higher US–Latin America trade would have multiplier effects on the demand for Canadian goods from both the US and Latin American markets, given increasing hemispheric linkages. This is particularly the case as there are significant levels of complementary trade in the region. In areas such as automobiles, electronics, food industries, and chemicals, much trade is complementary and the use of inputs from different countries tends to increase overall trade flows. At the micro level, this may also be reflected in intra-firm trade, which is strong between Canada and the US. Intra-firm trade is also becoming increasingly important in Latin America today.

I would like to also point out that geography and development of transportation routes contribute to tighter links between Canadian and hemispheric markets. Again, hemispheric free trade would maximize Canadian trade opportunities, as Canada would have more choices for covering integrated rather than fragmented markets in the region. Under hemispheric free trade, transportation routes to West, East, and Great Lake ports in Canada could be used more efficiently by shipping to markets which otherwise are not covered because of the high cost involved in serving small demand. This is particularly the case for agricultural products or other products that have to be exported in bulk.

With respect to short- to medium-term opportunities, Latin America is definitely a growing market for key Canadian exports, including computer-related products, banking services, telecommunication products, and agriculture and resource-based products. There are good reasons to think that higher economic growth in Latin America would be an important contributing factor to sustain the investment, employment, and production boom that Canada is presently experiencing in the production of fibre-optic materials (for internet connection), telecommunication products, and computer software and hardware. Latin America is modernizing, our urban population is large, and we have made progress in introducing sophisticated infrastructure and technologies.

Population size and demographic trends should be taken into account in more than one way when considering the bilateral trade relation between Canada and Latin America and the Caribbean. As we know, countries with young and large populations can provide an important short-term direct source of higher demand for imports. A statistical correlation has been observed in the US between demographic trends and firms' financial performances. We expect that under hemispheric free trade an increasing number of Canadian firms will be more exposed to Latin America's dynamic demographic trends. This issue is of particular importance if we take into account the slowdown in population growth in Canada and the implications that this has for economic growth.

Beyond trade and investment opportunities, Latin America has much to offer to Canada in other areas of international relations. It is a reality that Latin American and Caribbean countries and Canada have increased cooperation in international organizations, including at the Inter-American Development Bank (IDB). We have worked together on issues such as the orientation of lending programs, implementation and support of economic reforms, putting together rescue operations to deal with financial instability, and FTAA trade negotiations. On the latter, Canada has played a key role in hemispheric issues and has related to Latin American and Caribbean countries in a way not seen in the past. This interaction is very enriching for hemispheric relations and we have expectations that it will continue to be felt on other hemispheric issues.

Trade negotiations at the regional and multilateral levels can be seen, in particular, as an area where more cooperation between Canada and Latin America and the Caribbean may prove very important. Common positions may influence international events in new ways. One example is in the FTAA context: a powerful consensus has emerged to work towards the multilateral elimination of export subsidies for trade in agriculture and this view has been expressed as a hemispheric position in WTO discussions.

KEY CHALLENGES

What are the major challenges that may arise in the relationship Canada–Latin America and the Caribbean over the next few years? I am very optimistic about these exciting times in which our countries should come closer together. But we also have to be realistic about potential problems that can arise and ask how we can transform challenges into opportunities.

One challenge may be that, as we make progress towards free trade and market integration, we will naturally see increased competition in markets in the hemisphere and elsewhere. This is good news from the point of view of increased economic efficiency and should promote opportunities for all of us based on comparative and competitive advantages. We will need, however, efficient and practical dispute settlement procedures to solve normal disputes that arise from commerce. Also, the arguments we make today about the opportunities from free trade that would arise for all countries can only become a reality, particularly for the least-developed countries and disadvantaged regions, if proper infrastructure and technical support are put in place. The region also suffers from market failures in different sectors where information is poor and incomplete. Institutions throughout the region will need to be modernized, including the capacity for management of public policy. For many sectors and regions, discussion of proper adjustment mechanisms to make this process viable is also important. And there would be sectors, well-known to each country, where interest groups will resist change.

Another challenge we will face together is the problem, both in the private and public sectors, of transparency of procedures for doing business. Major efforts will be required to address this problem. However, technical cooperation, ongoing institutional reform programs, and the FTAA negotiations in the areas of government procurement, investment, and dispute settlement, as well as customs and business facilitation initiatives, should prove useful. Nevertheless, we will need to explore ways of developing an overall coherent approach on these matters.

We will also face the challenge of becoming accustomed to living closer together during the fluctuating of sometimes-unpredictable cycles of international markets. The recent financial crisis that began in Asia and spread to Russia and Brazil has demonstrated how rapidly financial crises can spread to many countries. Today, we have a good opportunity to reflect on the conditions under which, in the context of a free trade zone, we will face together the reality of these market forces. Macroeconomic policy consultation may also be an area where we may need to initiate discussion. Economic fluctuations also create the temptation to use discretionary measures that increase trade protection. If used, such measures would be very detrimental and send the wrong signal about a new era of hemispheric relations. The FTAA negotiations, once again, provide a good forum to discuss this matter.

Finally, I would like to emphasize that the IDB is committed to support economic reforms, including the major objective of opening up our economies to freer trade. Canada plays a major role within the Bank and has made important financial and intellectual contributions to all of our major initiatives. We are confident that the IDB and Canada will continue working closely together on the many projects that are transforming our hemisphere. Although the challenges and work ahead are enormous, by continuing to work together we can make our emerging hemispheric village a more prosperous and just place.

April 2000

International Financial Markets
The Prospects for Economic Growth and Stability

PAUL VOLCKER

It's an honour to be part of the Sylvia Ostry Lecture series. All through Sylvia Ostry's life she has thought it was her mission in life to make things better, in fact, to make the system better, to make the world economic system work better. Her vision and her influence are international.

There has been enormous progress in the development of freer trade in these past few decades. It's expanded with very little interruption and it certainly has reinforced growth in the world generally and particularly growth in the newer and emerging economies of East Asia. It's been a great help to the transitional countries of Europe and to parts of Latin America. Now we're facing a new round of trade negotiations. I'm not going to discuss them except to say that I know they're going to take a long time. They're not going to come to fruition very quickly, given the strong political pressures. There is the ironic picture of the United States taking protectionist measures, presumably in the defense of free trade negotiations. That is how convoluted and how difficult this area can be.

I want to consider other issues bearing on the prospects for economic growth and stability that seem to me to require a lot of attention. In the process, I'll try not to over-dramatize the situation in which we find ourselves either in the industrialized world or the emerging world.

The end of the Cold War and a lot of technological advance led to a huge amount of exuberance about the prospects of the world economy, about the prospects for opening markets, for the prospects, most particularly, I think, of emerging countries. There was a great sense of opportunity. Now, quite suddenly, a few years after financial markets were pretty much opened, we find ourselves with a sense of frustration. I think we are in a rather crucial testing period – testing the success of the model of democratic capitalism we all cited so strongly just a decade ago in greeting the prospect of a truly globalized economy. For all that great sense of exuberance, I think it's evident – read no further than the press, read no further than the reports on the International Monetary Fund (IMF) and the World Bank in September 2002 – that we now have lots of doubts and questions. Part of that, of course, is the demise of the great stock market bubble in the United States and elsewhere, but I don't think that's the most significant thing that's happened.

The fact is we had a virtual collapse of many of the Asian economies in 1997 and 1998. We have very sluggish performance, very difficult performance in Latin America now. There is the very great challenge of sustaining the growth of those East Asian economies. Only one of them – Korea – is anywhere near back to the growth path that it had before the financial markets were open. So it's no great wonder that people can begin raising questions about whether they've been sold a bill of goods or not in terms of the opening of markets.

I won't cast any doubt on the ultimate importance of open markets in supporting growth in the emerging world as well as in our own countries, but let me point out that those countries are more dependent upon trade, more dependent upon external finance, than we are in North America and Europe. It's only fairly recently – in the mid-1990s – that markets for finance in the emerging world became the norm.

There are all sorts of theoretical and practical arguments about how open financial markets in the world should be as a source of great strength to emerging economies; whether that is happening in reality is not entirely clear, to say the least. What we do know is that they have been victimized, if that's the right word, by enormous swings in capital flows. At first, in the midst of the exuberance in the mid-1990s and earlier, there was a big flow of capital toward East Asia and substantial flows into Latin America. Then there was the "Tequila Crisis" in Mexico that, in fact, was set up by an excessive flow of capital into Mexico. A couple of years later came the Asian crisis itself. In all these crises, there was a sudden reversal of capital flows, with the result that those economies were thrown into turmoil by very sharp depreciations in their exchange rates, very sharp in related increases and interest rates, and a situation that created a profound sense of recession right through much of Asia and, indeed, Latin America as well.

So we're left with a question. Is this just a phase, a learning experience, something we needed to pass through, or does it really raise serious questions about the benefits of Western-style open financial markets? Is it really essential that open financial markets become an integral part of a successful growth pattern for those countries? My answer to the latter question has to be yes. Potentially, over time, participation in world capital markets can and should pay large dividends for the developing world. However, for that to materialize, we're going to have to pay a lot more attention to some basic – what I take to be structural – problems, systemic problems in the financial system. The needed reforms are by no means, in my mind, limited to the emerging nations themselves.

Why do I think that? I think there is an important structural fact that we can't change overnight and in some sense won't change.

What we do know is that international financial markets are volatile. They've always been volatile. I have no expectation they will become less volatile. You can argue that modern technology and the speed of transportation and the ease of communication and exotic financing techniques may make them more volatile. I don't know whether that's true, but there's no reason to think that financial markets won't continue to have sharp cyclical swings and be sensitive to political and economic shock. We read about that almost every day in the news – and feel it in our own portfolios!

Generally we take the view, certainly we take the view in the United States, that that kind of volatility is a price we pay for the enormous advantages, the indispensable advantages, of open and competitive financial markets. It's part and parcel of the process of "creative destruction," to use the term so popular in 2002. It propels essential economic change and growth. Our experience pretty generally is that we can absorb that volatility without lasting damage to our economies.

It's a rather interesting phenomenon. We can have stock markets decline by 50 per cent or so and still have what was only a very mild recession, even with the additional complications of 9/11 and other things, and continue to grow. We have basically strong financial institutions and particularly stable political institutions. But even in our case we know there have been occasions when the imbalances and turbulences have been so great as to interfere with prospects for economic growth and even threaten political stability for an extended period. I think the 1890s and the early part of the twentieth century in the United States – particularly the 1920s and the subsequent 1930s in the United States – were examples of that. One of the interesting characteristics of both of those periods in my country and elsewhere is that they led to some rather fundamental reforms of the capitalistic system: anti-monopoly legislation, the Federal Reserve itself early in the century, and, in the 1930s, the Securities and Exchange Commission (SEC) and deposit insurance. Compulsory auditing of corporate accounts and other investor protections, all grew out of these major crises. But we survived them.

In contrast, take the case of the typical emerging economy. By their very nature, by their very size, they are structurally much more vulnerable to the vicissitudes of financial markets than nations in the developed world. This struck me particularly forcefully some years ago, but I could take other examples. I went to Argentina after the Mexican crisis in the mid-1990s and they asked me to look into the problems of the banking system. I was somewhat familiar with Argentina, but what struck me when I looked at it was that the total size of the Argentine banking system at that point was $40 billion. When I got back to New York, I ran into the chairman of the second-largest bank in Pittsburgh, Pennsylvania, and asked him, "How big is your bank?" He said, "$40 billion." That gives you some sense of relative size. I assure you that that bank in Pittsburgh, Pennsylvania, was being visited by an investment banker at least twice a week, telling them they were too small to survive in this modern, turbulent, globalized financial world.

So there we are with countries that are not only small in national terms but whose total financial markets are much smaller than the size of individual institutions in the industrialized world. Relatively marginal changes in the investment policies of these institutions can be a major destabilizing influence on the markets of emerging economies. One response to the crises has been to urge floating exchange rates as a means of absorbing the shock. But, when your external trade is 50 per cent of your GNP, which is not unusual for these small and open economies, you can't afford to be very blasé about your exchange rate. In combination with other disturbances – particularly loose swings in the interest rates – big changes in the exchange rates will create enormous economic problems. So we face the fact that major parts of this world simply don't have the institutions and the safeguards and the safety nets and the political stability that we are used to in this part of the world.

A typical reaction to the Asian crisis by Western officials and financial institutions alike, you may recall – and I'm not simplifying very much – was, "Well, you know, it's their fault. They don't have good American auditors. They don't follow generally accepted accounting principles (GAAP). They've got crony capitalism. They don't have enough transparency, they're not open enough." I had some doubts about those opinions at the time, and it is more than a little ironic to recall them in view of what is going on today. My central point is there are some basic structural issues here that go beyond those kinds of questions. I think the relevant metaphor for the emerging countries is a canoe in the ocean: it's fun when the sea is very calm, but if a storm arises – and it may arise from some distant area – you'd better get out of that canoe and into a bigger ship.

The problem is they can't get out of their canoe very easily. One of the results of the Asian and other crises – and it's a lasting reflection, in the sense of several years – is that the flow of capital has moved from the emerging world, ironically, to the developed world, and particularly to the United States. So we have, I think, an economically and also morally questionable situation. The richest, strongest economy in the world is sucking capital out of the poorest economies in the world that presumably need it for growth. Now what do we do?

I've already hinted that the long-term answer isn't going to be found in insulating those economies. If you think of controls on capital and money flow as a kind of permanent answer, I think you're at a dead end. Inevitably, that would place a drag on trade itself and it's certainly going to discourage any chance of getting sustained capital inflows. Perhaps worst of all, if you think of the kind of controls that would be required in today's world to insulate an economy financially, the result would be to feed corruption, which is a serious enough problem as it is.

I think we're going to have to find a solution in terms of further financial integration. That seems to be the inevitable and ultimate consequence of all the efforts to free trade that have been made through the years, with considerable success. What does it mean when I say we need to turn to further integration?

I want to touch on one area of a big, complicated problem that isn't going to be changed very quickly. That area is the exchange rate system or, as many people, including myself, characterize it, a lack of system. You know it's very fashionable in both the policy world and in the world of economists to say, "Well, we've got a system: everybody can do what he wants with their exchange rate. That's a system."

But there's a certain peculiarity in exchange rates. The very definition of an exchange rate is that there's another country at the other end. You cannot determine an exchange rate policy without determining somebody else's exchange rate policy. In fact, in a multilateral world, you simultaneously determine the exchange rate policy of a lot of countries. So I'm not sure that we have an adequate answer in basically saying that every country can do its thing. On the other hand, it is a very difficult thing to find a substitute for this kind of *laissez faire* approach. What I am convinced of is that we should not leave exchange rates entirely to the market. Beautiful as the textbook vision looks – and a whole generation of economists has now been schooled in those textbooks – with exchange rates moving gradually, adjusting to differences in inflation and income or external shocks and creating a new equilibrium over time – that lovely vision bears no relationship to any practical world we have seen over the past decade and more. That's as true, I must say, in the industrialized world as it is in the emerging world, although the changes are not so sharp and so disturbing.

We, in the United States and the European Community, have exports and imports a little more than 10 per cent of our GNP.

These days, changes in exchange rates of 50 per cent or even more are not comfortable but can be absorbed without upsetting the whole economy. That is not true for nations trading in the international market. Exchange rate swings of 50 or 60 per cent are not unusual in the free and open markets in the emerging world. I think that's endemic, as I suggested before, with the degree of volatility that's inherent in capital markets.

Let me conclude the point by saying, quite simply, that over time the inherent logic of a completely open trading system, and particularly a completely open financial system, is a common currency. We already see that logic at work within Europe. We see it to some extent as individual other countries cling to the euro or to the dollar. But we are left in a very uncomfortable position when the international system has not been rationalized and we are left with very big swings between the major currencies that inevitably disrupt the trade of smaller countries.

There is another part of the structural problem and it also leads to a conclusion that greater integration is part of the solution rather than the problem. The emerging world can achieve and reinforce the kind of stability they need through direct investment. Happily, direct investment has held up pretty well in the last few years, even when other forms of capital have been reversing and moving out of the emerging world into the United States and elsewhere.

It's long been known and praised that direct investment brings money, obviously, but also technology and management. It also brings other things that are particularly important and have increasing importance. It brings stability. It's not quite as easy to move out of direct investment as it is portfolio investment or stock investment. You have built a plant. You have inventory. You have a growing business and you have a continuing commitment to the country. All of that is stabilizing.

I refer to the tiny banks, relatively speaking, that these countries have had. It was not an accident that almost all the Argentine banks became foreign-owned because the independently owned Argentine banks knew that they could not withstand the potential pressures. The last piece put in place in the North America Free Trade Agreement (NAFTA) negotiations with Mexico was liberalization of the financial markets and, particularly, the possibility of foreign ownership of Mexican banks. There was finally a tortured compromise with a long phase-in. Within two years of when they got into trouble, the president of Mexico went to Europe and the United States urging, "Please buy one of our banks. We need some stability." There is not a major Mexican-owned bank left, including the biggest. It astounds me that even the biggest Mexican bank is now foreign-owned, but the consequence is, I think, an important additional degree of stability in Mexico.

This brings me to the problem of today. If direct investment brings stability, it can also bring good corporate practices, the kind of thing that we were advertising during the Asian crisis: good auditing, good accounting, good financial transparency, and lack of corruption. We sold that story pretty hard. I think there was some sympathy for it in other countries.

It's a hard thing to do. A lot of tradition, governmental structure, and business practices are ingrained. The best chance at making some progress, I think, may be through the example of well-run foreign investors and direct investors. But now what's happened? They look at the United States and say, "What about this Anglo Saxon model of capitalism? You've got some outrageous scandals. What's going on? Is it really the model we want? Is that what you were suggesting to us?"

I don't have to elaborate what we read in the press every day. The problems are not actually new. We've had recurrent problems of this sort in the past. We have obviously had really outrageous examples of pushing the envelope too far, of outright fraud, lurid examples of what can only be described as looting a corporation. But I don't think it's just a matter of "a few bad apples in the barrel." The outrageous behaviour is only an extreme manifestation of patterns that have become much too common and are aided and abetted by attitudes that almost inevitably develop, I think, when you have the kind of boom and bubble we have in our stock market. I think that phrase of Alan Greenspan's, "infectious greed," is a good description of what was going on.

Yesterday, before I came up here, I was talking to a fairly prominent Wall Streeter who's now off Wall Street. We were talking about the cultures and traditions and ethics of Wall Street. He made a rather sweeping and surprising statement: "What do you expect when business schools for decades have been teaching the only thing that counts, the only measure of success, is how to get your stock price up?" I'm afraid there is more truth in that than we like to admit. So my concern is that if we are going to deal not only with our own problems but are going to make some contribution to the effectiveness with which a globalized economy can aid and assist economic development, we'd better be serious about reform of corporate governance and financial reporting.

The good news here, and I think it is good news, is that the evidence is so outrageous that we have a political platform for change. I don't have any doubt that in every boardroom, every audit committee, every compensation committee in the United States, and probably in Canada as well, and in Europe too, directors are looking at their responsibilities a little differently. That's a good thing. I think it will have an impact. But I'm old enough and perhaps cynical enough to wonder whether it will last – whether it will outlast the declines in the stock market and the daily focus in the press. So, useful as that rethinking is, important as it is, I think we need to complement that with structural change and with legislation.

I have been most involved recently in the auditing side of things. In my seventh decade, I am not about to become a technical expert in auditing. But I have been exposed enough to our auditing firm, and to the auditing profession, to become convinced that the profession has – as part of huge multi-purpose consulting entities – lost its way. The big firms became so fixated on their desire to grow, their desire to be more highly compensated, that the auditing side became a relatively small part of the business and auditing independence and discipline weakened.

I was startled one day, when I was getting a little bit involved with Arthur Andersen, to see one of their marketing brochures. It had nine orange boxes on the first page (orange was Arthur Andersen's colour). One-half of one of nine boxes was auditing, which tells you something about where their mind was. Too often, there and elsewhere, auditing had become an entry into other businesses that they thought more interesting. At the same time, corporate clients were not going out of their way to insist upon good, probing audits. Instead, auditing came to be looked upon as a cost centre. At the same time, they were hiring and paying a lot of money to investment bankers and financial engineers to find their way around the accounting and tax rules.

Then there was the new profession of compensation consultants. It's not too much to say a certain dynamic took over. The client, by definition, is a first-class company, but you cannot be a first-class company unless your chief executive is paid above the median. Nobody's yet figured out how everybody can be above the median, but the effort to try imparts a certain momentum to compensation practices. In all this process, there is one peculiar thing about the auditing profession. It has a special responsibility. The auditors are mandated to serve the investor, not the particular corporate client, but the market. The auditor is the guard against false reporting and misrepresentation.

There can't be any doubt that the profession came under very heavy pressure and, relative to other business professions, they are not particularly well compensated. In time, they got conflicted and auditing standards were weakened. That is one area that I feel reasonably confident is going to be changed. It's not at all simple to be a good, disciplined auditor. But the problem has become clear and we now have the legislation that can provide the necessary oversight, that will stiffen the backbone and reinforce the discipline I think we now all understand we need in the auditing profession.

There are other problems. There's the executive compensation problem, there's the sheer complexity of markets, the sheer complexity of big multi-purpose financial institutions that inevitably have massive internal conflicts of interest. That is spectacularly true of stock analysts who have, to put it bluntly, in too many instances, become hand-maidens of investment bankers. That is now all laid out for everybody to see and that is an area where we are going to see changes.

I wasn't born yesterday. I know we can't get rid of all the conflicts of interest. There is always a possibility of legislative overkill. But I am more worried about the implementation of the legislation we now have. We have, frankly, let the Securities and Exchange Commission (SEC) run down. That is being repaired; I hope it's being repaired effectively. We have the new auditing oversight body, but that has become mired in a political fight about who gets appointed to that board. But I do think we are making real progress toward reform.

I want to add a few more radical thoughts as to what could be done further in the context of corporate governance in the United States. For one thing, I think the day of the "imperial" chief executive officer ought to be brought to an end. The preferred method of managing a large public company should include a non-executive chairman with one particular responsibility: the management of the board of directors. If the chief executive officer is also de facto manager of the board of directors, it's hard to conclude that that board is really independent, whatever the technicalities of the definition of independence. There is general agreement that non-executive directors should have regular opportunities for frank discussions among themselves about the management of the company. That may not make much difference nine years out of ten, but when a company gets in trouble and when the chief executive himself is perhaps the source of the trouble and the question of his tenure is at stake, I think it is very important to have some alternate point of leadership in a board of directors.

Just to be a little more radical, let me consider this question of stock options. This enormous increase in executive compensation in the United States is unquestionably driven by the popularity of stock options, particularly options granted at a fixed price. The conceptual rationale for stock options has been to align the incentives of management with the stockholder. But it hasn't turned out that way. I think the fixed price stock option has been so subject to abuse, and the temptations for abuse are so great, that there ought to be a strong prescription against fixed price stock options for large publicly owned companies.

My final radical point concerns making it possible for boards of directors, and particularly for auditing committees, to discharge the responsibilities that both principles of good governance and now the law assigns to them. Who has the knowledge, the time, the capacity, the desire among the members of a typical board of directors of a very complex large organization to effectively oversee the work of the internal auditors, the external auditors, to determine the pay of the external auditors, to hire and fire the external auditors, to maintain oversight over the internal financial reporting of the company? Not very many, I would suggest. So I think there is a real question of how we elect people to the board. Perhaps the stockholders should explicitly elect members of the auditing committee – men or women who already have the interest, the ability, and the willingness to do the kind of work that an auditing committee is asked to do. It is a job, in my opinion, that takes more than a meeting every few months, with maybe a phone call when a quarterly report is issued, or what often becomes a rather pro forma meeting with the external auditor.

I thought it appropriate to end with those tantalizing thoughts. But what can't be escaped is the larger issue. Corporate governance, corporate responsibility, is part and parcel of an effectively operating, open, free, global financial system. If democratic capitalism is going to be successful, it must work not only to our benefit but to the benefit of emerging countries. We are going to have to do a better job than we've done in the past. The good news is we are now well on the road toward doing that. The ability to respond, to make changes, to reform is, I believe, part of the genius of the American economic and political system.

October 2002

Contributors

MICHEL CAMDESSUS served as managing director and chair of the Executive Board of the International Monetary Fund (IMF) from 1987 to 2000. He continues to play an international role as UN Secretary General Kofi Annan's special envoy for the 2002 International Conference on Financing for Development, as head of the Panel on Financing Water Infrastructure, a financial taskforce for the World Water Forum, and as the representative of French President Jacques Chirac to the New Partnership for Africa's Development (NEPAD). Mr Camdessus is also Chair of the Board of the Centre d'études prospectives et d'information internationales (CEPII), France's leading institute for research on the international economy, president of the Semaines Sociales de France, and a member of the International Advisory Board of IESE, the graduate business school of the University of Navarra.

Mr Camdessus joined France's Ministry of Finance and Economic Policies in 1960. After serving as financial attaché to the French delegation at the European Economic Community in Brussels from 1966 to 1968, he returned to the Treasury and went on to become assistant director, deputy director, and then director. Mr Camdessus also served as chair of the Paris Club and chair of the

Monetary Committee of the European Economic Community. In 1983 he was named alternate governor of the IMF for France. In 1984 he was appointed first deputy governor and then governor of the Bank of France; the same year he was appointed governor of the IMF. He continued to serve as governor of the Bank of France until his appointment as managing director of the IMF in 1987.

JACQUES DELORS served as president of the European Commission from 1985 to 1995. With British Commissioner Lord Cockfield, he crafted and won approval of the Single European Act (1986), which laid the groundwork for the creation of a single EC market in 1993. Mr Delors also oversaw the transformation of the European Commission into the European Union, which moved the EC nations toward a single currency and greater cooperation on defense. In particular, the Maastricht Treaty, a work of the Delors Committee for Economic and Monetary Union (1988–89), led to the creation of the single European currency and paved the way for the Euro.

Since May 2000 Mr Delors has been president of the Council for Employment, Revenues and Social Cohesion (CERC), an independent organization mandated by law to give advice on the links between employment and revenues, distribution of revenues, and social inequality. He is currently chair of Notre Europe, a think tank established to study and research Europe's history and future prospects.

Jacques Delors began his professional career at the Banque de France – the French Federal Reserve. In 1979, he was elected member of the European Parliament and became chair of its committee on economic and monetary issues. From 1981 to 1984, he was finance minister in the first government under President François Mitterand. On the local level, he served in 1993 as mayor of Cliché Marcha.

Following his tenure as president of the European Commission, in 1996, Mr Delors served as chair of the UNESCO Commission on Education for the Twenty-First Century.

ENRIQUE V. IGLESIAS was first elected president of the Inter-American Development Bank in 1988 and in 2002 he was re-elected for his fourth five-year term.

In the years leading up to his election as president of the IDB, Mr Iglesias served as Uruguay's minister of Foreign Relations; executive secretary of the UN Economic Commission for Latin America and the Caribbean (ECLAC); secretary general of the 1981 UN Conference on New and Renewable Sources of Energy; and chair of the conference that launched the 1986 Uruguay Round of international trade negotiations. These negotiations led to the creation of the World Trade Organization, the successor to the General Agreements on Tariffs and Trade.

Mr Iglesias began his professional career in the private sector as managing director of the Bank Unión de Bancos del Uruguay. From 1964 to 1967 he was Uruguay's delegate to the Latin American Free Trade Association, ECLAC, and the Inter-American Committee of the Alliance for Progress. From 1966 to 1968 he served as president of Uruguay's Central Bank.

Mr Iglesias has taught economic development at Uruguay's Universidad de la República, served as director of the university's Institute of Economics, and was a member of the board of directors of the Latin American Council of Social Sciences (CLACSO). He presided over the United Nations Latin American and Caribbean Institute for Economic and Social Planning (ILPES) from 1967 to 1972. He has written numerous articles and papers on Latin American and Uruguayan economic issues, capital markets, external financing, and multilateralism and has received many honorary academic degrees and professional awards.

SADAKO OGATA was named co-chair of the Commission on Human Security in June 2001 and special representative of the Japanese prime minister for Afghanistan assistance in November 2001. Since May 2001 she has also served as a scholar-in-residence at the Ford Foundation in New York City. In 2002 Mrs Ogata was awarded both the J. William Fulbright Prize for International

Understanding and the Eleanor Roosevelt Val-Kill Medal. These honours and appointments follow her distinguished career as United Nations High Commissioner for Refugees, a post she held for three terms from 1990 to 2000.

In her long service to the international community, Mrs Ogata has been the independent expert of the United Nations Commission on Human Rights on the Human Rights Situation in Myanmar; the representative of Japan on the United Nations Commission on Human Rights; and chair of the Executive Board of UNICEF. In 1978 and 1979 she was envoy extraordinary and minister plenipotentiary at the Permanent Mission of Japan to the United Nations, having served as minister there from 1976 to 1978.

During a distinguished academic career, Mrs Ogata served as dean of the Faculty of Foreign Studies at Sophia University in Tokyo, where she had also directed the Institute of International Relations. Before joining the faculty at Sophia University, she was associate professor of diplomatic history and international relations at the International Christian University in Tokyo. From 1965 to 1974 she lectured in international relations at Tokyo's International Christian University and University of the Sacred Heart.

Mrs Ogata has also served on numerous government advisory councils, and boards of academic associations and foundations.

RENATO RUGGIERO served as director general of the World Trade Organization from 1995 to 1999. After his tenure at the WTO, Ambassador Ruggiero was appointed chairman of ENI, Italy's national energy company. He left that position to become vice chair of Schroder Salomon Smith Barney International and chair of Schroder Salomon Smith Barney Italy. In 2001 Ambassador Ruggiero was appointed minister for Foreign Affairs in the second government of Italian Prime Minister Silvio Berlusconi. In 2003, in addition to his role as vice chair of Citigroup's European Investment Bank, Schroder Salomon Smith Barney, Ambassador Ruggiero was appointed chair of Citigroup in Switzerland.

Ambassador Ruggiero entered the Italian diplomatic service in 1953. Throughout his career he has held numerous federal positions in the Italian government, including political advisor to the president of the European Commission; diplomatic advisor to the prime minister; chef de cabinet of two foreign ministers; director general for Economic Affairs at the Foreign Ministry in Rome; Italy's permanent representative to the European Community; personal representative of the prime minister for seven G7 summits; and chair of the Executive Committee of the OECD in Paris. During his tenure with the president of the European Commission, he participated in the development of the first European Economic and Monetary Union project and the official launch of the European Union project at the 1972 European Summit in Paris. In 1977 he assisted in the negotiations that led to the launch of the European Monetary System.

In recognition of his contributions to public life, the president of the Italian Republic made Ambassador Ruggiero a knight of the Grand Cross. Many foreign governments have also recognized his work in the cause of international trade and diplomacy.

PAUL VOLCKER served as chair of the Board of Governors of the US Federal Reserve System from 1979 to 1987. First appointed by President Jimmy Carter, he was re-appointed by President Ronald Reagan in 1983. Upon completion of his second term as Federal Reserve Chair in 1987, Mr Volcker returned to private life, becoming chair of Wolfensohn & Co. Many of his current activities reflect his strong interest in improving the professionalism and effectiveness of public service, and he is currently chair of the second National Commission on the Public Service. A former chair of the Trilateral Commission, he also serves on a number of other public and private advisory boards, including the Japan Society, the American Council on Germany, the American Assembly, the Group of Thirty, the International House, and the Institute for International Economics. In addition to his other official duties, Mr Volcker chairs the Board of Trustees of the International Accounting Standards Committee and serves as co-chair of the Financial Services Volunteer Corps, a not-for-profit private-public partnership whose mission is to help build the sound banking and financial systems required by countries seeking to develop transparent market-oriented economies.

In the course of his career, Mr Volcker worked in the federal government for almost thirty years, serving in high office under five presidents. He served as under secretary of the Treasury for Monetary Affairs from 1969 to 1974 and president of the Federal Reserve Bank of New York from 1975 to 1979. As chair of the first National Commission on the Public Service in 1988, he established himself as the nation's most pre-eminent advocate for the revitalization of the public service.

Mr Volcker has received honorary degrees from some fifty universities.

PETER G. WHITE is executive vice-president of the Ravelston Corporation and of Argus Corporation, and a director of the Fraser Institute and a number of major international corporations.

Among his various roles in the public sector, Mr White has served as special assistant to the Hon. Daniel Johnson, premier of Quebec; as a member of the Rt. Hon. Brian Mulroney's transition team and as his principal secretary; as founding chair of the Public Policy Forum; as president of the Council for Canadian Unity during the 1995 Quebec Referendum; and as immediate past chair of the Institute for Research on Public Policy (IRPP).

In his extensive private sector service, Mr White was co-founder – with Conrad Black and David Radler – of the Sterling Newspaper group, which later became a wholly owned subsidiary of Hollinger Inc., a director of the Argus group of companies, chair, president, and CEO of Domgroup Ltd, and publisher of *Saturday Night Magazine.*

On the international scene, Mr White was named chevalier de l'Ordre National de la Légion d'Honneur by the president of France for his efforts in developing strong economic ties between the two countries as president of the Canada-France Business Club and long-time president and later chair of the Canadian Institute of International Affairs.

THE HON. MICHAEL WILSON is chair and CEO Canada of UBS Global Asset Management (Canada) and chair of the Canadian Council for Public-Private Partnerships, the Mental Health Implementation Task Force for Toronto and Peel, and the Global Business and Economic Roundtable on Addiction and Mental Health. He also serves as a director of a number of companies and on the boards of such professional and community organizations as the Canadian NeuroScience Partnership, the Centre for Addiction and Mental Health, the Arthritis Society, The Aspen Institute, and the Institute for the Americas.

Between 1979 and 1993 Michael Wilson was a member of Parliament and held a number of Cabinet portfolios, including minister of State for International Trade, minister of Finance, minister of Industry, Science, and Technology, and minister for International Trade.

Prior to has career in public life, Mr Wilson was executive vice-president of Dominion Securities Limited. He was also founding chair of Michael Wilson International, which provided advice and assistance to companies seeking to expand their international business activities.

Michael Wilson's civic and voluntary leadership garnered him an Outstanding Volunteer Award from the National Society of Fundraising Executives and in 2002 he was given the Canadian Council of Christians and Jews' Human Relations Award.